PRAISE FOR AFTERBURNER SEMINARS

"Outstanding . . . the entire sales team and guests were overwhelmed by the correlation between flying a combat mission and the sales and business mission our people face each week."

—Charles C. Gerrish,
director, sales development, Johnson & Johnson

"Over the years we have had many different types of presentations, speakers, workshops, etc., but nothing that has produced the results that Afterburner has given us."

—W. Andrew McKenna,
president, midwest division, The Home Depot

"The entire Afterburner team did an outstanding job of relating our current business conditions to a military analogy and mission strategy. Feedback from our attendees was outstanding."

—Robert C. Hunter,
president and CEO, PepsiCo Systems

"WOW! Did you ever strike a nerve! Not only was our field sales organization impressed with your presentation—our sales managers are all requesting an outline . . . so they can reinforce the message in the upcoming months."

—Kay Guiseppe,
vice president, vendor relations,
McKesson General Medical

"[Afterburner Seminars] delivered 'bombs on time and on target,' which made our mission a TOTAL SUCCESS!!!"

—Jamie "Impact" McDevitt,
total systems management executive,
southern marketplace, IBM Global Service

BUSINESS IS
COMBAT

BUSINESS IS
COMBAT

A FIGHTER PILOT'S GUIDE TO WINNING
IN MODERN BUSINESS WARFARE

JAMES D. MURPHY

ReganBooks
An Imprint of HarperCollinsPublishers

A hardcover edition of this book was published by ReganBooks, an imprint of HarperCollins Publishers, in 2000.

First paperback edition published 2001.

Designed by William Ruoto

Printed on acid-free paper

Library of Congress Cataloging-in-Publication Data has been applied for.

ISBN 0-06-098829-0 (pbk.)

01 02 03 04 05 ❖/RRD 10 9 8 7 6 5 4 3 2 1

To Mom and Dad, who gave me the confidence to tackle life's opportunities no matter how difficult they seemed. Your belief in me has helped me soar higher than you will know—thank you.

I love you!

CONTENTS

ACKNOWLEDGMENTS

There are so many people who have helped, coached, inspired, and guided me through my life's journey.

To all of you I am grateful.

To my family, Mom, Dad, Traci, and Cheryl, for the greatest gift of all—family and a place I can call home.

To my friends Doug Keeney and Bill Butler for "tweaking" my rough manuscript, and for your great coaching through this process.

Thanks to my agent, Marc Reede—you're a great wingman!

To John Gamble for encouraging me ten years ago to start this journey.

To Delilah Syperda, Dave Bogage, and everyone at The Home Depot for the chance of a lifetime!

To Bob Smiland and Ron Bogdanovich for giving me the chance to learn business execution on the front lines—you guys are the best!

Special thanks to my partners, Anthony Bourke and George Dragush, and the entire Afterburner Team for giving me the opportunity to give a voice to the things you do day in and day out, and whose work, generosity, ideas, and time have supported me in so many ways.

To Hank and Angie Davis, thank you for all the days and nights of brainstorming!

To Rebecca, my soul mate, thanks for believing in me and my dreams. Your support has been my inspiration!

INTRODUCTION

In 1990, Saddam Hussein ordered the invasion of Kuwait, and in so doing put into motion the allied response known as Operation Desert Storm. In that memorably televised operation, one image was particularly memorable to me: Positioning himself behind one of the runways used by our jets, a cameraman caught a spectacular shot of twenty-four F–16s lining up for a tactical formation take-off. Now, tactical formation takeoffs are a little unusual. For one thing, the jets don't wait until the runway is clear. Instead, they use what is called minimum interval spacing—one jet starts rolling as another nears liftoff. Once they start, off they go, one after the other with no delay, each pilot pushing up the throttles—creating white-hot flames from the afterburners—until the entire package is in the air. It is a stirring display of air power. Even through the TV screen you could smell the JP–4 jet fuel and feel the ground shake from the thunder of the exhaust.

Now, imagine the same image, but with one tiny change: one of the pilots running toward the ramp with a donut clenched in his teeth, coffee spilling from the cup in his hand, yelling "Wait! Wait! I got held up in traffic!"

It wouldn't happen. Each of those twenty-four pilots knew the package was an abort if he didn't perform his individual part. No one was late. No one forgot to wake up on time. The only thing that might have kept one of those pilots from hitting his mark was a massive coronary, and even then he'd have been checking his watch.

The point is, the execution of that extraordinary mission came down to people. For all its bristling hardware, the most powerful asset of the United States Air Force is the same as the most powerful asset of any company—people. Jets don't fly without pilots, and if pilots aren't ready to man their jets, the mission fails. And if too many missions fail, battles are lost and, sooner or later, so is the war. The same holds true for any company in the world, large or small. Today, more than ever, business is combat. And without an empowered sales force, without enthusiastic marketing, without customer service people who care about their product or services, there's no doubt—you may win a battle here and there, but you'll lose the war.

The question is how to do it. How do you turn your customer service force into twenty-four fighter pilots ready, willing, and able to leap into the sky and engage the enemy? How do you empower your sales and marketing people so completely that they're willing to risk life and limb for your company? There have been plenty of books about organizational structure, organizational behavior, the principles of effective management, and strategic planning in business. This book is about *execution*—about orienting you and your company toward the successful execution of individual missions. It outlines a people-first approach to business that aligns the company behind, not in front of, the individual missions undertaken by the individuals of the company. And its mission is to show companies how to give their employees all the tools they need not only to accomplish their daily tasks, but to excel.

What a powerful one-two punch—to have the entire organization aligned behind you, and to have the tools to win. I should know: I was an F–15 fighter pilot for the United States Air Force. Every time I strapped on my jet I had the vast resources of the entire Air Force aligned behind me like the shaft of a spear. I had an array of mechanics, handlers, and weaponeers making sure I was good to go. I had an intelligence organization on the ground to brief me on my threats and their weapons. I had weather crews updating me on the environmental picture fully and clearly. I had airborne tankers aloft if I needed fuel. I had AWACS airplanes above me monitoring every moving thing in my airspace. I had fellow pilots in a wide range of aircraft protecting me by looking to kill enemy missile sites and anti-aircraft batteries. Best of all, I had years of advanced training behind me. I knew my jet, I knew my mission, and I had the tools to execute it flawlessly. Every time I left the runway, I had what I needed in my hands, at my back, and at the ready.

That's what this book is about—tools. Not just any tools, but fighter pilot tools. Tools that can help you win in the combat of business. The lessons in *Business Is Combat* show you how to apply the time-tested disciplines and doctrines of the most forward-leaning organization in the world—the fighter pilot community— to your business today. It is a distillation of countless carefully conceived strategies, procedures, methods, and standards that have turned tens of thousands of ordinary men and women into victorious fighter pilots. I know firsthand, because I've been through the system myself. I went from farm boy to fighter pilot in two years. When I started I barely knew how to fly; before I was done I was a flight lead and an instructor pilot in the most advanced fighter jet in the world.

I no longer fly the F–15. Today I spend my time training tens of thousands of people a year to apply the disciplines I learned in the cockpit to their own lives and in their own companies. I try to teach them everything I know about teamwork, planning, preparation, communication, discipline, observation, execution, debriefing—everything they need to know to improve their daily win ratios. It doesn't matter whether I'm working with an accounting firm, a packaged goods manufacturer, an airline, a mass market retailer, a law firm, or an emerging technology company. It doesn't matter what size the company is, how far its leaders went in school, or how much money its employees make. The same principles apply. Why? Ultimately, business and combat both come down to absolutes—winning or losing, putting food on your table or losing it to another person, being ready for the unexpected, taking advantage of a rapidly changing environment, or being left behind. But the tools I recommend have been forged in the heat of air combat. In the lightning-fast, unpredictable world of the digital millennium, the tools designed to keep a fighter pilot alive aren't just relevant—they're indispensable.

In the chapters that follow, I will demonstrate that the most effective way to harness the incredible—and sometimes hidden—power of people is to focus on execution. That's the fighter pilot way. That's the Air Force way. All you need are the right tools. Read on. And get ready to win.

FROM FARM BOY
TO FIGHTER PILOT

It's midnight in Panama. I'm lying in my cot, trying to catch some sleep, but I can't do it. My mind is going a mile a minute and my body is restless. I toss and turn and stare up at the roof of my cinder-block bunker; my uniform is drenched in sweat. The birds and animals that were invisible during the day are alive now, calling one another in the dark. Though the sun is long gone, it's 95 degrees. I can feel the humidity with my hand.

I'm in Central America, an F–15 pilot with the 116th Fighter Wing of the Georgia Air National Guard. We're here on an anti-narcotics mission. We've been tasked with intercepting unannounced intruders into Panamanian airspace, the assumption being that they're bad guys—drug smugglers. To do this, we're sitting five-minute strip alert, which means that if we're called suddenly, we have to be airborne in five minutes. That's why I'm lying awake in the middle of the night in a steaming jungle. It's my turn to fly the alert. I'm too excited. Adrenaline is coursing through my body. My jet is sitting 100 feet away on the ramp of our jungle airstrip, fueled, armed, and ready to go. Cocked, as we say: The radios are even pretuned to the right frequencies.

Now all I have to do is get some sleep.

To put this in perspective, let me explain that this is my first real mission. Until now, it's been all practice, training hops and basic fighter maneuvers (BFM). Realistic for sure, but not the real thing. Well, tonight it's the real thing. Tonight I'll be flying in a hostile environment with a fully armed F–15 for the United States Air Force. This time lives are hanging in the balance.

Gradually I surrender to bone-deep fatigue and fall asleep. My body has crashed from days of overexcitement, and it's absolute bliss. But then, just as soon as I'm locked into deep REM sleep, the klaxon blasts through the ready room and the call goes out to scramble the jets! My eyes shoot open, but I have no idea where I am. What is this noise, this heat, these pools of sweat? *Intruder!*

As my mind comes swimming up slowly from the bottom of the ocean, I react. I recognize the outline of two F–15s ahead of me in the dark and run in the general direction of mine. I hit the ladder with my right foot, scramble up, and take my seat in the cockpit. I take a deep breath and look at the panel. *I'm racing the clock*, I think; *I've got to get a move on. I've got about four minutes to get this bird in the air.*

But I'm not with it. I'm groggy. It's totally dark. The blackness in the cockpit is confusing. Now, on an F–15 there are dozens of buttons to push and switches to flip before you can start the engines and get airborne. If you had all the time in the world, it wouldn't be a problem. But doing it quickly is another story. You have to activate all the proper switches in the proper sequence, starting on the left side of the cockpit and working your way around to the right. When I first started flying, the fastest time I ever had—dead engine to airborne—was twenty minutes. After hundreds of repetitions, I whittled the time down to fifteen minutes. Then to ten, then to five. I can still hear my instructors yelling, "Murph, move it! You've got to do better than that!"

Well, right then on the ramp in Panama I needed to do better than that. I looked sideways over at my flight lead, to see how he was doing. I looked back at my panel. I started feeling my way around the cockpit. I began to recognize things, instruments, handles, parts of the jet. And then the whole training scenario came flooding over me like a cool spring rain. Wham! I went on automatic. I reached down and pulled the JFS (jet fuel starter) handle, which initiates the start sequence in the F–15. I heard the familiar sound of the central gearbox engaging and the slow rotation of the engine's compressor blades. My engines came to life, the lights on the panel started to glow. Suddenly things started to happen. My hands started to move with authority, my motions became precise and efficient. I worked over the switches. I read indicator lights. The jet's systems started to align. The INS (inertial navigation system) came up to speed. All weapons tested, tuned, ready to roll. Engines normal. In two and one-half minutes I was taxiing, and thirty seconds later I was pushing up the throttles on 42,000 pounds of pure thrust, thundering down the runway with the long lick of afterburner flames trailing behind me. My heart was racing. I leaned forward in my shoulder harness. It was time to engage the enemy.

I'd been a fighter pilot since the hot July day in 1990 when I reported for duty to the 116th Fighter Wing of the Georgia Air National Guard. I got to fly the hottest jet in the hangar: the McDonnell Douglas F–15 Eagle, a twin afterburning beast of a jet that can routinely cruise at 1,200 miles per hour. But six years earlier, if you'd told me that's what I'd be doing, no one would have been more surprised than I. My plan was to be a professional baseball player. Four years of college, a few years in the minors, then join my father's company—that was it. Sure, I'd loved airplanes as a child. But F–15s? Never occurred to me. I didn't even have a pilot's license. I was just an ordinary guy from a small country town in Kentucky, with no interest in the military whatsoever. Things do change.

FOUL BALL

All through my school years, my real passion was sports. I picked up any kind of ball I could get my hands on: You couldn't keep me busy enough. Fortunately I was good enough to make the teams, and by the time I was in high school I was playing every season—football in the fall, basketball in the winter, and baseball in the spring.

One thing you have to know about me is that I've never been accused of lacking confidence or enthusiasm. Give me an opportunity and I'll work myself silly to take advantage of it. Tell me it can't be done, and I'll show you it can be. As it happened, I excelled in baseball, so much so that I won a scholarship to play at Eckerd College in St. Petersburg, Florida. Well, that was the opportunity I wanted. Not only was I going to play well for Eckerd, I decided that I was going to parlay my brilliant play all the way up to the major leagues. Baseball became my sole focus and purpose in life. I practiced harder, played harder, and put out more than anyone on the team. I wanted to be the best player in Eckerd's history.

Luckily, things took off right away. Even before I finished my freshman year, some professional scouts saw me and talked me into transferring to a junior college so I would be eligible for the professional draft a year earlier than in a four-year college. Who was I to argue? I left Eckerd and transferred to Pearl River Junior College in Mississippi and had a great season—until the major leagues passed me up in the draft. No draft? Well, things weren't as bad as they seemed. I still had two years of eligibility, and I was recruited by the University of Kentucky. I signed with UK and played out my dream as a collegiate ball player. There would be no major leagues for Jim Murphy, but I had two wonderful seasons in the bluegrass country. I was happy.

A New Order

During my sophomore year in college, my dad and my uncle started a distribution company called Triple M Business Products. They offered thousands of office products, including Toshiba's line of copy machines. Triple M fast became a presence in my life. My phone calls home were about Triple M. On holidays and vacations, my dad and I talked about Triple M. I spent weekends walking up and down shelves of inventory. I think I knew more about office products by the time I was a senior in college than half the seasoned professionals my dad had working for him.

The summer before graduation, I worked for Triple M as a salesman-in-training. Of course, I took a lot of good-natured ribbing about being the boss's son, but my coworkers quieted down after my numbers started coming in. I poured myself into my job, hustling from one account to the next. I shot up to number four, then number two in overall sales, and even closed the very first copier sale for the entire company. Maybe I had a knack for it or maybe it was my youthful enthusiasm, but whatever the reason, by the end of the summer I was the top salesman in the whole company.

So it was no surprise that on the day I got my diploma from the University of Kentucky, my father and my uncle Joe were waiting at the end of the graduation aisle with a job offer. I was thrilled to have the chance to show them what I really could do.

When I joined Triple M full-time, I hit the ground running like Pete Rose barreling into second base. I immediately regained my spot as the top sales rep in the company; soon I was promoted to field trainer, and became responsible for training all the new salesmen. Eventually I took over the home office in Louisville. I had a full staff—service techs, salespeople, and office personnel—and I was only twenty-three years old.

I learned a lot about business in those years. Most of all I learned about people. As a manager you inevitably encounter every personality type, both in your own company and among your customers. You quickly learn that people are motivated differently and respond to different things. People are alternately weak and strong, decisive and tentative, bold and meek. I was constantly amazed at the varieties of human nature. I observed it all—not always satisfied with what I saw—and filed it away for future reference.

The Lure of Flight

The Kentucky Air National Guard is about as cool as it gets. In 1987, it had a ramp full of RF–4C Phantoms, the meanest-looking planes in the sky. The Phantom isn't a sleek jet and it certainly isn't brand-new, but when it comes down to a street fight, you'd rather be in an F–4 than any other plane in the sky.

That year, I happened to meet a fellow who was about to start flying those F–4 Phantoms. One Saturday afternoon he suggested we go out to the Air National Guard base just to tour around. I was in a why-not? kind of mood, so off we went. At the base we met a fighter pilot who must have read my mind: "Hey," he asked, "how would you like to sit in the cockpit of an F–4?" Would I?

I loved selling; I even loved copiers. But I had never really been sure if it was all entirely right for me. By that point in my life, I have to admit, I was looking around, thinking about options, wondering what to do with myself. Well, sitting in that F–4 was a life-changing experience. As soon as I grabbed the canopy rails and let myself down into the cockpit, I thought, *This feels right.* A voice in my head said, *Maybe this is what you're going to do. Maybe this is what you were born to do.* To this day I can't explain it. There had been nothing in my background to lead me in this direction. Nobody in my family had even been in the military. But the feeling! That view out of the cockpit! A big smile creased my face. This was my turning point. I was going to be a pilot.

After I left the base, I started taking flying lessons at Bowman Field in Louisville, Kentucky, starting out in little Cessna 152s. I circled the pattern endlessly, practiced my touch-and-go landings. I learned all I could. But being the person I am, pretty soon I started asking about military aviation. Cessnas were nice, but the F–4s were the majors.

Now, becoming a fighter pilot is about as difficult as making it in the majors, and since I'd fallen flat on my face once, you'd think I would have learned. But no, I started visiting the recruiters. The Air Force recruiter wasn't encouraging; he told me I had to be an engineer with a 3.0 grade point average to get into pilot training. Scratch that.

So I went next door and talked to the Navy. They were a lot more interested. They gave me a test, which I guess I did well on, and within a few weeks they'd called to offer me a slot. I was stunned.

I ran back to Triple M and told my father and uncle about my decision—but as word spread, so did an undercurrent of shock and disappointment. I was twenty-three, setting sales records, running the home office like it had never been run before, and all of a sudden *Oh, by the way, I'm leaving next week to fly jets off an aircraft car-*

rier. Instead of pats on the back, I was greeted by long faces and furtive glances. I guess I knew why. We really had turned into a great team; breaking up the office was not a happy prospect. Triple M meant a lot to all of us. We had built it into something that was growing by leaps and bounds. And, as excited as I was, I still wasn't sure I really wanted to leave all that behind.

Luckily, fate would bring me face-to-face with a new mentor/ coach in Major Jim Riechenbach of the Georgia Air National Guard. As Major Riechenbach showed me, the guard was a bargain made in heaven: I could fly jets but still pursue a business career. I said, "Where do I go to sign up?"

Well, it wasn't nearly as easy as I thought. In fact, it would be two years before the Georgia Guard unit had an opening. There had been almost 300 original applicants, and they had narrowed it down to eight guys. I was one of the eight. After interviews, motor skills tests, psych tests, physicals, and a grilling in front of the whole board, they made me their selectee. "Do you drink beer?" they asked. You bet I did. I was on my way to Officers Training School and a whole new life.

The Air Force Way

Nothing in my background prepared me for the military way. I didn't know how to salute; how to recognize rank; or how to walk, talk, or chew gum military-style. I just wanted to fly jets, but that was enough to propel me forward through the Academy of Military Sciences in Knoxville; the United States Air Force Flight Screening School in Hondo, Texas; the Undergraduate Pilot Training in Del Rio, Texas; the Fighter Lead-in School at Holloman Air Force Base in New Mexico; and finally the F–15 training at Luke Air Force Base in Phoenix. I went from hotshot salesman to pilot-in-training, from coat and tie to green flight suits. And I loved it.

In fact, what I was responding to was the Air Force way. Without expecting it, I had stepped into the battle-honed system that had made America the undisputed master of the skies. Each step in my education was part of an elaborate selection process that squeezed out the less proficient candidates, then squeezed out the ones who lacked commitment, then squeezed out the pilots who couldn't become team players, then iced the showoffs, until the Air Force had a class of thirty ready to graduate, among whom just three or four would go on to advanced fighter school. I was at the top of my class. I was among those blessed with good eyesight and quick reflexes, with an aptitude for the three-dimensional environment of air combat, and with an ability to function within a team. I earned the opportunity to fly fighters, and my jet was the best the Air Force had—the F–15 Eagle.

I was finally living my major league dream—only the uniform was different.

Getting Back to Business

Maybe it was because I had some business experience before I became a fighter pilot, or maybe it was just another one of those flashes, but one night I suddenly sat bolt upright in my bed and thought, *Boy, if I had had training like this in the copier business, I would have been unstoppable.* I started jotting down notes. The organization. The discipline. The planning. The attitude. The process that turned me and thousands of other people into fighter pilots was nothing short of a textbook for the creation of cutting-edge business warriors. The light bulb over my head was flashing a message: *Everything I have just learned can be applied to business.*

Just as I had when I slipped into that F–4, I went back to sleep knowing that I was about to make a career change. I was ready to go back into business. Not just any business. I was going to teach the principles of fighter pilot training to business men and women. I even had a name for it—Afterburner Seminars.

Practicing What We Preach

As always, there is rarely a direct line from one career to another. In fact, it would be four years before I started Afterburner Seminars. In between, however, I was given a chance to put my thoughts and my training into practice. In 1992, I gave a talk to a Young Presidents Organization (YPO) group that was visiting my squadron. My topic was applying fighter pilot principles to every-day business. After the presentation a man named Bob Smiland of the Smiland Paint Company came up to the lectern. He asked about my business background, then told me about his business. He said, "I've got a company that's rapidly growing, and in about two years we're going to be in the southeastern United States. I'm looking for young, leaning-forward guys like you to help run our company." I was flattered. Afterward I sent him a thank-you note, then forgot the meeting ever took place.

I continued to fly the F–15. Then, almost two years to the day after that meeting, I got a phone call. It was a guy named Scott Lyons from New Jersey looking for me. I called him back. "Mr. Lyons, this is Captain Jim Murphy, 116th Fighter Wing, return-ing your call."

"Yeah, Jim. My name is Scott Lyons and I'm with Conco Paint Company. Bob Smiland told me to give you a call. I just wanted to know if we could get together sometime soon?"

I had totally forgotten about Bob Smiland and his company. I just said, "Well, Scott, I think you may have the wrong Jim Murphy. I'm not really sure I know what you're talking about."

He said, "Well, you graduated from the University of Kentucky. You played baseball there on scholarship. Now you're flying for the Air National Guard, F–15s."

I said, "Yeah, you've got the right Jim Murphy."

True to form, my life was about to change again.

Back in Sales—And Putting My Ideas to Work

Within a matter of weeks, I signed a contract to become the director of sales and training for Conco Paint Company, the com-pany Smiland Paint had become. My job was to run and train a sales force, take care of manufacturing and marketing, and handle the Home Depot account. I continued to fly the F–15 as a tradi-tional weekender in the Guard.

For two years I traveled the United States developing our sales plan, expanding into new markets, working closely with Home Depot merchandisers and Home Depot store managers—doing all I could to grow the Conco business. I made a conscious effort to apply what I had learned as a fighter pilot: to gather intelligence on my competition the way I had studied the MiG–29; to plan my customer presentations as thoroughly as I had my mission in the squadron; to debrief each meeting as seriously as our own post-flight debriefs. This was a real-world test for me. Could my fighter pilot know-how make me a better businessman? I felt sure it could. If I was wrong, I would know it all too soon.

The results were spectacular. Two years later, I was running a division that had grown from $5 million in sales to $50 million. I had more products in more stores than anyone dreamed. And I knew the reasons for my success. It was the teamwork. The attention to detail. Conco had learned to take on a mission with the same spirit and drive that the Air Force engendered in its F–15 pilots. We knew our line of products. We knew the competition. We presented ourselves with credibility, commitment, and real enthusiasm for our customers. More important, we as a sales team were helping one another, supporting one another, encouraging one another to be winners. Just the way it worked in the squadron, I could see it working for Conco.

With this experience under my belt, I resigned in 1995 to start the company I had visualized for years, Afterburner Seminars—a company that was going to teach businesses the fighter pilot disciplines.

Today we count some of the finest corporations in America—from Home Depot to State Farm Insurance, from Dell Computers to the Marriott Corporation—as Afterburner Seminars clients. We have thirty-eight facilitators who do training across the United States. We have taught senior managers, customer sales and service representatives—even entire divisions. We have learned from our clients as often as they have learned the fighter pilot way from us.

I was a farm boy. I became a fighter pilot. Now my team and I teach thousands of people a year how to be fighter pilot strong and savvy in the world of business. We give people new tools for their lives and their businesses, tools that help them stay ahead of their tasks, and to know what to do when they don't. If you take these lessons on board, you'll find they'll help you attack your missions with the calm and confident attitude that has characterized a half-century of military flight. They will transform you into a business fighter pilot. And they will help you move confidently ahead of the competition at the ultra-smooth speed of sound.

2

IN THE BEGINNING: VALUES

David Ogilvy was a great ad man. He created now-classic advertising campaigns for Hathaway shirts, Rolls-Royce automobiles, and Shell gasoline. He also wrote three books, *Confessions of an Advertising Man, Ogilvy on Advertising,* and *Blood, Brains and Beer.* All were probably as close to best-sellers as such books can be. But they were originally designed to pass on the Ogilvy & Mather culture to new employees. The books describe the great heritage of this venerable agency, the much-talked-about campaigns that defined its philosophy of advertising, the sales successes clients and agency shared, and the standards of conduct and professionalism that were crucial to its success. It didn't take long for new hires to learn Ogilvy & Mather's values, and everything that followed was built on this understanding.

This chapter is about values. It comes this early because the setting of standards, practices, policies, and expectations—the immersion in corporate values—must take place before anything else can occur. Without a deliberate communication of a company's fundamental parameters, people are forced to absorb what they can from what they see, and that's not always the best way.

The military does a good job of inculcating its standards, practices, and all-important heritage to its new members. In the Air Force, new recruits never see an F–15. Instead, they have the common values and expectations of the Air Force drilled into them until this fundamental understanding is complete. Afterward, all the training, all the evolving standards of performance, and all the awards and successes are built on these first planks in the organizational platform.

Setting the standards for any company is a unique process. So many variables are specific to each individual company that it is difficult to generalize. But certain broad, basic standards do exist, which have been proven to work in almost every kind of company. Most of them merge the needs of the individual with the overall objectives of the group. The Air Force has done a particularly good job of preserving the vitally important asset of individual creativity within its overall need to operate as a group. This has given Air Force pilots a set of values and character traits that any corporate culture would envy. As you choose the best way to establish your company's values, give some thought to the following seven elements of the fighter pilot world—elements that embody the values of the Air Force. They are the bedrock on which the chapters to come are built.

FLYING SOLO IS NOT A SOLO ACT

There's only one seat in the F–15 Eagle. It's just you at the controls. If anything goes wrong, it's up to you to handle it. But I learned something incredibly important on the way to becoming a fighter pilot: Flying is not a solo act. Flying is a group effort. It is the product of a team of people—pilots and maintainers, air traffic controllers and weaponeers. You all have to work together, or you're likely to die when you come up against a Russian SU–27 fighter jet.

Becoming a fighter pilot was one of the most intense life experiences I have ever had, and I learned as much about how to work effectively with people as I did about how to splash a MiG. I discovered that there was power in the group, and it showed itself in the form of three specific group attributes.

THERE'S MORE TO GETTING ALONG
THAN GETTING ALONG

First of all, at the heart of any good flight squadron is *camaraderie*. The heat of the job bonds pilots together unlike any other group I have experienced. This bond makes the job more than just a job. There is a level of caring and mutual support that you just don't find in the traditional workplace, or even on a baseball team. In the fighter pilot community, everyone tries as hard as possible to keep the group safe, to keep the group proficient, and to help the group win. This doesn't happen by accident. The Air Force forces you to work as a group. When I fly in an air-to-air competition, my entire squadron is graded on the basis of my performance. Conversely, I'm graded on the performance of my maintainers and weaponeers. We either work together and it shows, or we die as a group. The Air Force sets the standard—we will work well as a group—and it is up to us to make it happen. Sure, we have our moments of competition and politics, but when it's fightin' time we have a deeply embedded comradeship. Once you experience this, you'll want to re-create it everywhere in your life.

Teamwork is also at the heart of an effective squadron, and not just in the way you see it on posters. We learn to believe in teamwork as fundamentally as we believe in the stars and the moon and the sky itself. The math is simple: Two airplanes are more effective than one; four are more effective than two. But within that math are some subtleties. For instance, the formations we fly—that is, the relative positions of our aircraft to one another—are designed not only to let us deliver overwhelming firepower forward, but to enable us to defend one another against enemy attack from any direction. In this kind of formation, it is imperative to yield personal defense in favor of the group's defense. You can get a sense of this if you remember the great bomber formations of World War II: Those tightly bunched B–17s may have looked like an easy target, but it was a foolish German Bf–109 pilot who didn't stay clear of the hundreds of guns pointing *outward* from the formation.

The power of individuals merging their interests with those of others for the sake of the group—that is the trademark of teamwork, and the secret of military success. And no group can truly work as one without an understanding of *common goals.* Common goals are what turn any group into a force to be reckoned with. The underlying power of a fighter group is predicated on agreement—on the objective of the mission, on the strategy that will accomplish the mission, and on the tactics and teamwork that will put that mission into action. There can be no equivocation, no second-guessing, no doubts among the participants. There must be only zealous agreement, belief, and confidence. Again, this is difficult to find on a ball team, or in a company. There are always those who care only for their personal statistics. After two years in pilot training, my ego was still intact—nothing wrong with a fighter pilot having an ego—but it was spliced into a knot of teamwork and caring that I'd never known in my sporting days.

These three attributes—camaraderie, teamwork, and common goals—are the attributes of an effective group. They can be combined, practiced, and integrated into your corporate value system. Many companies routinely include group dynamics training during their national sales meetings. By far, teamwork exercises are the most powerful and emotional parts of our Afterburner Seminars. Just remember that the objective is not to turn people into unthinking cogs in a machine. Within a team structure, any successful company will place a premium on personal imagination, personal skills, and, most of all, adaptability. What's important is to forge a group whose members will all lend their best individual efforts to the greater good.

THE DOGMA OF INDIVIDUAL DEVELOPMENT

Fighter pilots operate in the most complicated environment of any job in the world. They have to think on a three-dimensional level, in three-dimensional space. They have to speak to different communications sources while straining under nine times their body weight just to stay conscious.

There are certain instinctive, God-given traits that make assimilation into the jet-pilot world a lot smoother. Good eyesight, physical strength, and quick reflexes are crucial attributes. So, too, is a competitive, ambitious personality. But fighter pilots aren't bred—they're made. Not every World War II ace had perfect eyesight or nimble reflexes. In fact, one post–Korean War study found that the only common denominator among the aces was a little experience hunting with a rifle. These men were *trained* to be jet pilots. Believe it or not, the process of Air Force pilot training can actually create an enhanced, more adroit mind through teaching and training—and can also create a higher-performing individual through psychological development. The process also results in four highly desirable individual attributes: *discipline*, *attention to detail*, *confidence*, and a *sense of duty*.

THE FINAL FOUR

Once, after a conference in Denver, a corporate manager came up to me and cried on my shoulder. "Murph," he said, "you can't imagine how frustrating it is in our business." I nodded and asked what he meant. His answer didn't surprise me. "I'd pay twice the going wage if people would only show up for work," he answered. "If they would only show up!"

All companies want their employees to honor, willingly and enthusiastically, the demands of *discipline*—the kind of personal discipline that makes you show up for work every day. But, as any sociologist can tell you, there are forces in modern Western culture that have eroded the value placed on discipline.

That's not a problem in the military. It has changed and modernized, but discipline is still at the heart of its training. It starts the very first morning of the first day of Officers Training School. You get up and you have your first inspection. If there is a piece of lint in the sink, you're going to get reprimanded for that. I went from having one of the messiest bedrooms of any teenager to worrying about whether I had a speck of dirt on my bunk and wondering if the hanger spacing in my closet was exactly three inches apart. After months of this, after months wondering what it had to do with flying a jet, I stopped asking why, and simply did. The development of a disciplined mind is about nothing more than harnessing your personal will and applying it to the job at hand.

Generations of Americans from all walks of life have found personal strength and success because the military life taught them an important lesson about the value of a disciplined mind. For fighter pilots, the importance of personal discipline is obvious. There are no sloppy veteran pilots in the fighter community. There are too many life-threatening events happening in the cockpit for a disorderly mind to manage.

Discipline can be developed on the corporate level as easily as on the pilot level. David Ogilvy was demanding about the quality of his company's work. He sent out scolding notes if he didn't like an ad. He wrote suggestions for improvements. He started company-wide newsletters. He instituted awards. All of this was designed to recognize those people who followed the Ogilvy & Mather disciplines. Further, not only did he link the clients' sales to company awards, he also exhorted endless research into the factors that made good—or bad—advertising. He laid out a disciplined approach to advertising at the agency's inception, and it permeated the organization from that day forward.

Discipline finds its ultimate expression in *attention to detail*. There is no part of pilot training, from the lowest to the highest levels, in which attention to detail is not hammered into one's head. Attention to detail not only makes you a better fighter pilot, it keeps you alive. Often as not, it's the small things that'll kill you—a little switch in the cockpit you forgot to flick, or an ejection seat left unarmed. Similarly, little things mean a lot in business—a typo in a proposal, misspelling a prospect's name, a sales sample left behind in the car. It's easy to talk about the big picture, but the hard work is in the details. As you'll see, discipline, alertness, and attention to every detail are the only things that stand between a pilot and a smoking hole in the ground. The Air Force drives that point home with ferocity. You can, too, with your own standards and policies.

While a wash-out mentality is an inevitable part of selecting the best pilots for jet-fighter duty, the Air Force has learned, over years of training, that aiming to kick someone out of the program is less desirable than inculcating the kind of *confidence* that can help keep him in. For most pilots-in-training, there comes a point when confidence suddenly blooms. For me, it came like a surge of adrenaline: I saw things more clearly, my hands moved the stick with more certainty, and all at once I felt a certain mastery over myself and my jet. This transformation came about not through some internal maturation on my own, but rather because the Air Force system had cleverly built me up through a series of small successes, imperceptible at first, that had a sudden, cumulative effect.

The very same thing can happen with your company. Throughout my early days at Triple M, I noticed the improvement in my presentations and my sales gains. It wasn't anything earth-shaking. But as one success built on another I reached higher, I reached for more, until almost without realizing it I had actually sold that first $1,295 copier. Payday was two days later, and instead of merely handing me my $200 commission check in passing, the sales director gathered the entire company, made me stand on a chair, and presented the check with a flourish. And I thought he'd hardly noticed. My confidence soared.

In addition to camaraderie, attention to detail, and confidence, there's one last trait that should find a place in your corporate value system. If there's anything all fighter pilots have in common, it is a *sense of duty*. No one forced us to become fighter pilots. Quite the opposite: We pleaded with the recruiters to get in, and we fought for our spots. Once we made it through training and became pilots, though, our motivations shifted. We were no longer flying to get through a flight test. We were flying because it was our duty to fly. We had made a personal commitment to do the work we pledged to do when we signed up, and we were obliged to honor that pledge.

We learn about duty in the Air Force. And what we mean by duty is different from blind allegiance: We have the leeway to question an illegal or immoral order. But when we joined up we chose to take responsibility for the completion of our duties, even if it should mean we fly at the risk of life or limb. And duty shouldn't be a hard thing to instill in the employees of your company—yet for many companies it's a priority that goes overlooked.

A sense of duty can be conveyed by teaching your culture, sharing your heritage, setting out for new employees the successes and failures you've encountered along the way, as well as the importance of your goals in years to come. Highlight the great performers in your company and memorialize them for years to come. Create awards for individual or group achievement. Give your employees a sense that there's something bigger at stake than their hours and their paychecks, just as the Air Force gives its pilots something bigger than the thrill of a jet. Bring your people along, help develop them, align them with the company and the company with them. In the end, you'll find your people will rise to the occasion and deliver just what the company needs—camaraderie, a sense of teamwork, willingness to operate under common goals, with personal discipline, attention to detail, confidence—and a sense of duty.

SUMMARY

The fighter pilot community is a homogeneous group. They may have come in the front door as individuals, but they come out as a group. They hold certain values in common—values that are important to keep in mind as you learn more about being a business fighter pilot.

Remember:

1. There is **camaraderie** within a successful group—a genuine personal connection forged in hours of training together.

2. **Teamwork**, not personal goals, defines the way a group goes about its business.

3. The group acts as one because its members share **common goals**. Its mission goals and plans are universally understood, valued equally by all.

4. On an individual level, each group member prides himself on **personal discipline**. Utter control of the mind and the emotions keeps everybody alive.

5. Discipline is expressed through **attention to detail**.

6. Pilots walk, talk, and act with **confidence**, and members of any successful group should, too. Uncertainty melts away as training and values set in.

7. At the core of every group should be a **sense of duty**—an obligation to fulfill the oaths and promises made when the wings were pinned on.

3

LEANING FORWARD:
THE FIGHTER PILOT WAY

Have you ever heard anyone say that business is war? A motivational speaker, for instance, or one of the many business gurus on television?

I'm here to tell you it's not true. Business isn't war; business is combat. You may think I'm splitting hairs, but I'm not. War and combat are very different things. War is the United States versus Iraq. Combat is an F–15 against a MiG–29. War is an army, combat is a soldier. War is AT&T versus Sprint. Combat is one salesperson going against another for that one sale.

As a fighter pilot, I don't fight wars. I go head-to-head in aerial combat with MiG–29s. If I execute correctly, I may win. And if enough of the pilots on my side win, we'll help win the war. But believe me, when I'm flying head-to-head, I don't think about submarines or the ground pounders below me. It's just me and that MiG, turning and burning in a three-dimensional battlefield until someone gives up the geometry, lines up a shot, and blows the other guy out of the sky.

Isn't that the way it is in business? A salesperson at Home Depot isn't fighting a war to dominate the national do-it-yourself category. The salesperson is there to make sure that every customer comes away convinced that Home Depot is the best place he's ever shopped. That's combat. Personal. One-on-one.

For a fighter pilot, combat begins and ends with personal execution. If I win my engagement one-on-one, and my wingman wins his engagement one-on-one, and if the others win theirs, we'll win the war. It's the same in the trenches. One soldier, one rifle. Our overall victory is based on the sum of our one-on-one engagements.

It's the same in business. Business is combat between you and him, not us and them. Either Zurich sells the insurance policy or it loses the business to another agent. Either Dell puts a computer on my desktop, or another brand gets on there instead.

BUSINESS IS COMBAT

Now let's take it one step further. Business isn't *like* combat; business *is* combat. Make no mistake about this. There are winners and losers. In my business, one fighter pilot flies home, the other is a memory. Business is the same. Business involves a set of mutually exclusive outcomes, and those outcomes are based on how well each individual executes his job. There's only one first mortgage on a home, one pizza on the dinner table, one beverage in the glass. Every day you and I fight to be *the* one, the product or service people choose to have. Victory, one-on-one, is all or nothing.

I am going to turn you into a modern business warrior, a fighter pilot equipped in every way to fight and win the vital battles that are a daily part of your business life. Your transformation from sheep to lion will require a change in your attitude, and that change involves your understanding that business really is combat, in the most visceral and urgent sense. To win, you must be absolutely prepared. Absolutely determined. So absolutely ready that you're leaning forward in your shoulder harness, restlessly waiting for the next sales call, the next walk-in customer, the next client meeting.

I want you to understand that every action you take and every decision you make is extremely important, and that the results of your daily combat are 100 percent essential to your success in life and to your company's success in business. Look at it the way we do in the fighter pilot community—execution can make the difference between life and death. That's the way I think when I strap on an F–15, and that's the way I think when I walk into my office. I want to be the winner, the victor, the person working for the company with the hottest stock or the greatest product or the reputation for the best salespeople. And guess what? That begins and ends with me.

THE UNITED STATES AIR FORCE

No other organization in the world, civilian or military, has structured itself as successfully, trained its people as appropriately, or supported its objectives as thoroughly as the United States Air Force. Everything it does is designed to make its front-line pilots winners, to empower the individual in the cockpit to plan and execute a mission flawlessly, to think quickly, to react quickly, to be prepared for endless contingencies, and to win. In today's rapid-fire high-tech e-business world, where technology changes before the naked eye and customer service is king, who could be better trained than someone who routinely flies at Mach 2? Every one of us in the fighter community deals with a fast-changing, chaotic, task-saturated world where even the smallest mistake, the slightest oversight, or the tiniest opening for the competition can mean death.

But there's more to it than that. The real genius of fighter pilot training is this: Long ago, largely through trial and error, the Air Force discovered the truths, the processes, the personal requirements that were necessary to turn almost anyone into a flexible-thinking, leaning-forward, confident, winning fighter pilot. If Air Force training can turn a farm boy into flight lead in a $30 million supersonic fighter—and they've done it with tens of thousands of other men and women—it can turn you into the combat victor you should be.

WORLD WAR II

Much has been written about the generation that fought and won World War II. Consider the situation in 1941. We were a nation intent on staying on the sidelines, weighed down by the Great Depression, not truly certain how we would go about fighting a war if we got into it. Our opponents, on the other hand, were formidable. Their many and powerful war machines were manned by battle-hardened troops with years of experience. In Europe, an unbroken string of victories had led the Germans to the eastern edge of the English Channel; in the Pacific, the Japanese were on our doorstep at Pearl Harbor.

All the more amazing, we didn't even *have* a freestanding air force at that point. Our pilots were part of the Army. And yet to win the war in Europe, we had to sweep the skies free of steely-eyed Luftwaffe pilots who already had hundreds of air-to-air victories to their credit.

It seemed to be a recipe for disaster. So what did we do? We took 30,000 young men out of their everyday lives and put them into a flight training program. When that was over, we gave them our P–51 Mustangs and P–38 Lightnings and P–47 Thunderbolts and sent them overseas. And guess what? One by one our farm boys flew their P–51s against the Luftwaffe's Bf–109 aces, and one by one they won. Everyday people, most of whom had never once given a thought to being in the military, went over to Europe and took on an aggressor nation that had years of experience expanding the Nazi empire from one end of Europe to the other, and won. In less than a year, we absolutely dominated the skies.

A few years ago, we did it again. In 1991, an entirely new generation of ordinary Americans was tested in air combat, this time against Saddam Hussein, an aggressor who had the world's fifth-largest army, layers of deadly accurate missile defenses, and an air force equipped with the latest Soviet and French fighters, the MiG–29 and the F–1. As we climbed into our jets and headed over to the Persian Gulf, we heard the loud boasts that American blood would flow like rivers.

To give this some perspective, you must remember that our fighter pilots were no more battle-hardened in 1991 than they were in 1941. Most military fighter pilots spend less than ten years in the service. Prior to 1991, we weren't engaged in significant combat anywhere in the world, so most of the pilots we sent to the Middle East were inexperienced Joes and Janes (in fact, many of them were weekend warriors, Air National Guard pilots). The Iraqis, on the other hand, had been on a war footing for years. Air combat? It was a daily prospect. Americans? They live a cushy life; send 'em over! And what happened? Well, you know that story. Once again we dominated the skies. In fact, we won so thoroughly that it may have been the most one-sided victory in the history of air combat.

The point is this: The long winning streak of the United States Air Force didn't happen by accident, or by luck. It is the deliberate result of the Air Force system that takes an average person and, through training, transforms him into someone who can take on an important job and execute it flawlessly, even in the spinning, turning chaos that characterizes air combat. It is a system that has been thought out, dissected, modified, reengineered, and perpetuated by generations of aviators who have put it into practice. It is a system that strives for perfection in every aspect of its construction—from cutting-edge machinery filled with the latest technology to training programs that leave nothing to chance; from an organization with all the logistical elements necessary to support people in the field, to leadership that has vision and the skill to communicate that vision with a sense of urgency.

The Air Force is playing the ultimate high-stakes game, and its doctrines, training procedures, and conduct are built around one absolute—winning. Handling whatever is thrown at you. *Our people will win*: That's the message. *Nothing short of that is acceptable.*

How would you like your company to feel that way, to act that way, and to perform that way? How would you like to be able to handle your environment better, adapt to change smoothly, field objections as calmly and effortlessly as Joe DiMaggio in center field? How would you like to feel so empowered, so prepared, so confident that you cannot lose? You can. It's all in the training.

BUSINESS THROUGH THE EYES OF A FIGHTER PILOT

Some months ago I walked into the offices of a small firm in the southeast. As I waited for my appointment, I made my way back to the mailroom, just the way I used to as a copier salesman. Now, remember, I hadn't sold copiers for ten years—but as I rounded the corner I saw their copier and I felt that surge again. Yes, it was the competition, my old competition. I fished one of my father's Triple M business cards out of my wallet and wedged it into the service window.

Old habits die hard, don't they?

ONE-ON-ONE

When I was a Toshiba copier salesman, my competition wasn't the Xerox Corporation. My competition was the Xerox copier salesmen in my territory. My concerns had nothing to do with whether Xerox stock was moving up or down, or whether Toshiba should build a new manufacturing plant. My concern was whether the Xerox sales force was better prepared than I was. Whether it had the stuff to take a customer away from me. Had the salespeople done their research? Did they know how many copies the prospect made each month, what kind of machine he used, how long his lease was? Did they know the pros and cons of my Toshiba equipment? Did they know me, my personality, and how I sell? Did they make friends with the receptionist and the boss's assistant? If they knew all that and did all that, then they were seriously prepared to take me on, and I needed to be concerned. They were about to put their fork into my steak.

On the other hand, I liked to think I made them worry. I liked to think I was better prepared, better equipped, and better motivated than my adversary. That's how I felt, anyway. I would get into my car in the morning, and even before the door was shut, I was planning my first sales call, rehearsing my facts, my presentation, my information, what-if-ing the contingencies. I can't remember a day when I left my home or office unprepared for combat. To me, it was always a battle against the other salesperson for one customer.

That's the fighter pilot way. That's what we call *leaning forward*. To get up in the morning gunning for the competition, eager to get into the office, anxious for the doors to open and anxious for the first customer to walk in and come up to you and ask about the difference between this and that, because you know—you *know*—you're better prepared than anyone else.

I can't tell you just what I was after when I slipped that card onto the copy machine. But I can tell you this: Once you embrace the fighter pilot way, you'll be the most effective, loyal, empowered individual your company ever had. You'll be stunned by how dedicated you've become. You'll wonder how you got so good at doing your job, why you like it so much. You'll wonder what came over you, how you got to this state of mind that makes you so thoroughly, totally focused on just one thing—winning the combat engagements of business.

Business at the Speed of Sound

To help you see how this works for you, let's compare our lives and see if we have common ground. Let me tell you about being a fighter pilot. A fighter pilot operates in one of the most task-saturated environments in the world. Before I climb into a jet, I have to learn all the latest technology, both my own and my enemy's. I need to know my enemy's habits, patterns, and capabilities. I need to know his jet's performance, turn rates, engine thrust, and everything that has to do with his radar and weapons systems. Then I have to know my own mission objective, its overall strategy, and my individual tactics within our formation. Once I get in the air, I'm in motion. Both of my hands are moving about the cockpit— one on the stick, one on the throttles. My eyes are darting about, constantly sweeping 350 crucial switches and dials, scanning the sky around me, all while the airplane is knifing through the sky at twice the speed of sound, slamming me with G pressures so great I have to do breathing techniques to stay conscious. I have other people out there, too, so I need to communicate by radio with my three wingmen, get intel by radio from AWACS, check my radar for bogeys, fly perfect formation to check the my wingman's six o'clock, and not hit the ground while I'm turning and burning in reaction to the bandit who's intent on killing me.

Does this sound like your business life? No? Well, think again. Once you've got your uniform on and you head to work in the morning, you're task-saturated, too. You've got to stay ahead of the competition on the technology front. You've got to know your competition's strengths and weaknesses. You've got to know your mission objective and your role in it. You've got to implement the new plans and procedures that just came down from the home office. Your phone is ringing off the hook. You've got ten faxes and twenty e-mails to return. Your spouse calls and your child is sick and needs to be picked up from school early. There's a meeting in fifteen minutes and your printer isn't working. Two people call in from their cars, they're stuck in traffic, and now you have to do their parts of the presentation. Your flight to Pittsburgh tomorrow just got canceled and twenty people have to be rescheduled.

Still think I have a tougher job than you? Sounds like we both have more or less the same job. Only I have an edge—I have the right attitude. And here are a few of the rules that help pilots like me maintain that attitude in any situation.

Rule #1: It doesn't matter if you're flying upside down or right side up.

Handle it. Change is good.

All right, we've established that we're both task-saturated. The question is, are we equally prepared to handle it? Let's examine the simplest concept—change. For fighter pilots, the environment in which we work changes by the second. Consider a typical mission. One minute I can be flying at Mach 1 (728 miles per hour at sea level), 500 feet above a hot desert floor. The next minute I can be rolling over on my back and flying inverted over a 12,000-foot mountain with two feet of snow on it, while dodging a thunder-storm off to my left. On the other side I'll end up over a lush green valley. That's how quickly the physical environment I fly in and around changes. But I don't think of it as a burden. Quite the opposite: I expect change, embrace it, adapt to it. Change is opportunity. We train to expect it and we train to use it to our advantage. We plug it into our flight simulators and throw it into our mock combat exercises. We learn to love change, to harness it. Because change always leaves the door open for improvement.

Consider the business environment you work in. Has it changed in the last few years? I'll bet it has. Are there more global competitors for the same market dollars you want? Is your workforce smaller and more flexible than it was? Are decisions being made faster than ever before? Are you personally being asked to do more in less time? Are your customers' expectations changing? If you're a manufacturer, are your fabrication practices totally different now, and has that affected your inventory and shipping structure? The Internet has probably become a huge factor in your business; if it hasn't yet, it will.

The question is this: Are you hiding from change, resisting it, rationalizing the status quo, or are you going with it, anticipating it, letting it propel you into new opportunities? Change can generate a tremendous amount of energy. Are you harnessing new energy, or are you consuming energy trying to fight it? I may not want a mountain in the middle of my flight path, but I'd be crazy not to pull up, wouldn't I? On the other hand, maybe I can use that mountain to my advantage, to mask my jet from the enemy's radar and lay in wait for the opportunity to pounce.

Look at how well the most staid, old-fashioned of companies have adapted successfully to change. I'm talking about the Baby Bells, like BellSouth. For decades they sold a very simple service—voice telephony, delivered through twisted copper wires, jammed into the side of every home in America. Did they foresee cellular phones? Video on demand? Internet on-ramps? The 500-channel universe of cable TV? Did they foresee digital answering services, voice mail, pagers, and caller ID?

Not at first, but when consumers said they wanted to be free of the wire—when they got a whiff of the potential of new digital services—did BellSouth whine and moan and let down its guard and open the door for an agile competitor to pick off business? Not on your life. The Baby Bells embraced the change. They saw digital as a vital new business opportunity, one that could spawn an infinite number of new products, services, and revenue streams. They fueled the energy of change with products that met or exceeded customer expectations. They harnessed the energy of change and let it propel their business forward. Twisted copper wires? Okay. But digital! Let's deliver interactive voice mail boxes, worldwide pagers, fifty channels of service—even buy up some of the cable companies and take command of that second wire into the home. Now they have entirely new lines of business, with robust new revenue streams augmenting their traditional hard-wired world.

BellSouth could have resisted this change. It could have decided that its core business was just fine as it was. But it believed it could put these changes to use, and it did—to the extent that basic phone service is the now the last thing you'll see them advertising.

Less well-known, but equally challenging, has been the constant pace of change in the food industry. Until the mid–1980s, the only alternatives to the standard fare of meat and potatoes were a handful of rather tasteless, low-calorie foods. If you wanted to reduce your fat intake and still enjoy tasty prepackaged foods, you were simply out of luck. That all changed with the emergence of fat and cholesterol consciousness. No longer was it enough to flag the words "Low Calorie" across a package. Now a product had to be "Low Fat" and "Cholesterol Free" to be healthy. It was a shift that propelled the development of countless new products and count-less new line extensions: reduced fat cookies, guiltless corn chips, fat-free desserts. Even specially bred cattle and branded lean beef offerings gained space in the supermarkets. The public's desire for low-calorie foods expanded to low-fat foods. Now, all this change could have sounded like a death knell for the snack-food industry, or for that matter for fast-food chains. Sure, they could have thrown their money into new packaging and new ad campaigns as a way of defending their territory and defusing the momentum of the "health nuts." Instead, they allowed the momentum of change to propel their sales upward. KFC introduced oven-roasted chicken. McDonald's introduced a line of entree salads and meatless burgers. Frito-Lay introduced Olestra. Kellogg's introduced reduced-fat granola cereals. You can even buy reduced-fat candy bars and ice cream!

That's the way to do it. That's how to put that oncoming mountain to work for you. And once you learn how to do that instinctively—to believe that you can turn any change to your advantage—you'll go *looking* for change, the way we pilots do. That's the only way to move ahead.

Rule #2: Don't fire last year's missile against this year's MiG.

I hate to do homework. I'm no different from any other fighter pilot. I'd rather strap on my F-15, light the afterburners, pull up the gear, get vertical, and punch big blue holes in the sky. Who wouldn't?

But I also like to stay alive. And I can't do that by ignoring changes in technology. I can't beat the new Russian SU–27 Flanker with last year's missiles. So I spend a lot of time in the intel vault (our library of classified information) updating myself on the latest radar software, avionics, and missile enhancements. Believe me, I'm happy to do it. I may hate to hit the books, but we fighter pilots appreciate the technology edge. Advanced technology is our ace in the hole, and we'll take every advantage we can get.

There's nothing more high-tech than an F-15 fighter jet. It's a $30 million hot rod with a supercomputer in it. It flies twice the speed of sound, shoots AMRAAM missiles with launch-and-leave capability, and sports a radar system that can see the gold fillings in an Iraqi's teeth at forty miles. I sit in it even today and marvel at its capabilities.

But even more amazing than that is the fact that the pilots who fly these things learn to do it in only seventeen months. Let me trace this progression, because it demonstrates the capacity we all have for adapting to technological change.

I started my journey to the Eagle in a 180-horsepower, piston-engined aircraft called a Cessna 172. (The military calls it a T–41.) We had one knob for the gas, one button on the control stick (for the radio), and ten or twelve flight instruments. It could do 120 miles per hour on a good day with a strong tailwind.

As soon as the Air Force saw that I could fly this little plane it pulled it out from under me and threw me into a jet! That doesn't happen in civilian aviation, where you crawl from a single-engine rating to a high-performance rating to a multi-engine rating and then maybe to jets. It can take years in the civilian world. Not in the Air Force. Their experience has shown that pushing people quickly up the learning curve is better. So, boom! You're in jets.

First I flew a T–37, a docile little 6,000-pound, twin-engine jet that looks like your grandfather designed it. Then the Air Force yanked that out from under me and threw me into a twin-afterburning super-sonic jet called the T–38. What a change: Now I had to start thinking fast. I had to stay ahead of the jet, plan my next move while I was in the middle of the previous one, all the while traveling at nine miles a minute toward my target.

Then, just as I got comfortable with the T–38, I was thrown into fighter training—and suddenly flying became a minor part of the whole equation. I had to become, essentially, an operator of technology. I had to view the jet as a high-speed platform from which tactics could be employed and weapons could be delivered. Instead of aviation skills, my training took a sharp and permanent turn toward technology, especially in air-to-air armament delivery. In fact, I was now being graded more on my savvy with the tech-nologies than on my flying skills.

Let me give you an example. Missiles are pure technology. When I first got into the F–15, our primary missiles were the AIM–7 Sparrow and the AIM–9 Sidewinder. At that time they were 100 percent cutting-edge. The Sparrow was one of the first true BVR (beyond visual range) missiles. To complement this missile, we had radar technology that could identify a target as friend or foe before a pilot actually saw it.

However, there were limitations. You could lock up only one target at a time (STT—single target tracking), and the target had to be illuminated for the whole TOF (time of flight) of the missile. If the target was flying in a four-ship formation and you wanted to take them all out, you had to have four F–15s, each locking on a separate target. This is a process we call *sorting*. But sorting was also our Achilles' heel: As soon as the enemy learned about all this new technology, it started to fly in tightly bunched defensive formations called *resolution cells*, designed to confuse our radars and make sorting difficult by making four planes look like one. This forced us to fly in closer to get a good shot, but by that time we had lost our technological advantage and had moved into the enemy's WEZ (weapons engagement zone).

Along came the AMRAAM missile to solve these problems, but with it we had to learn a whole new set of skills. The AMRAAM is a force-multiplying missile. Instead of needing four F–15s to take out four MiGs, one F–15 could now carry up to eight AMRAAMs, launch all eight of them on different targets, and never get within visual range of the threat. No matter how tightly the enemy flew its formation, each missile's guidance system sorted it out and honed in on just one MiG. It was a great weapon, but it required new tactics, new training, new thinking, and plenty of time with the manuals. Back to class.

Here's the point: No one said adapting to new technology would be easy. In fact, technology shifts are often weeding-out points for organizations, companies, and people. Why? Because technology and the employment techniques needed to use it are often difficult to learn. They force you to change. But new technology can give you the competitive advantage, so if you don't embrace it, you're less useful to the organization. I've seen it happen: When the new AMRAAM missiles came along, there were some fighter pilots who embraced the new technology, and some who resisted it. In fact, even some of the best fighter pilots in my squadron didn't make the change all that well: They'd been our top performers, but when the AMRAAM came along, they were more likely to revert to the old Sparrow techniques—which no longer worked. The less-experienced guys, who weren't so set in their ways, adapted to the AMRAAM more easily. They started beating the veterans in mock engagements—and soon, in that subtle shifting of power that accompanies change, the younger guys took over the squadron. They became the flight leaders and the instructor pilots, and the older guys became wingmen. Some even retired, unable to keep pace with the new tactics and the new environment in which we operated.

From the first day of pilot training through the last day as a fighter pilot, the fighter pilot community forces you to adapt to a world of constantly changing technology. It doesn't let you hide behind a busy schedule or too many weeks on the road or years of experience. You must adapt to it or you'll wash out—it's that simple. If you aren't in step with the new tech, you lose.

By the same token, today's businesses can't afford to float technology-resistant employees forever. If you aren't computer-literate by now, get literate *tonight*. If you aren't cruising the Internet, turn your browser on and get started. You're losing the battle. Technology, in the form of bar-code readers, infrared pricing systems, digital communication and message delivery, portable PCs, mailing software, the Internet, and so on, represents the single largest change in business today. Not only must you know how to use it, but you must know how to use it to your company's advantage.

Look at UPS. For years the drivers in those big brown trucks were weight lifters: they carried "dumb" boxes and hurried from one delivery to the next. Then along came modems, bar codes, and bar-code scanners, and suddenly the UPS driver was handling "smart" packages that could tell a hand-held scanner where it originated, where it was going, when it was delivered, and who signed for it. The UPS driver became a technologically empowered data collector, not just a weight lifter. The entire UPS system, and its battle-readiness in the competition with Federal Express and the other package delivery services, depended on the driver learning the new technology. Either that driver adapted and became a winner in his daily combat with the competition—or he was looking for a new job.

The key to weathering changes in technology, put simply, is to commit to it: Learn it, and train yourself and others with it, and do it eagerly and quickly. It's easy for a fighter pilot like me to appreciate this: I see how technology keeps pilots alive, so I take it absolutely seriously. It's not so obvious in business—not at first. But start to fall behind, and pretty soon you'll be wondering where your next meal is coming from. Never deny yourself even the smallest advantage. Embrace change. Do it as an individual, and as a company. If you don't, it's plain suicide.

Rule #3: The threat always changes.

The third advantage we have as fighter pilots is that we always expect the competitive threat to change. We watch for change. The very last thing we want is to be ambushed in a surprise attack, to be unprepared when called to action. We didn't know Iraq would invade Kuwait. But we had a training scenario for a Middle East war. We were ready.

In the fighter pilot world we don't have competitors. We have threats. Ten years ago I trained to do battle against the Soviet Union. I knew exactly where its fighter bases were. I knew its aircraft and their performance parameters. I knew the Soviet air tactics and procedures. I knew my areas of responsibility and the pilots I would fly against.

In 1989, my world changed. Down came the Berlin Wall, out went the Soviet Union, in came Russia and a dozen new nation-states. The massive air-to-air engagement we anticipated over the Barents Sea had been instantly replaced by the possibility of a number of small, fast-unfolding skirmishes in a half-dozen environments around the globe. The equipment I would fight against was now varied—not just Russian MiGs and SU–27s but French-built Mirages, Chinese jets, even old F–14s sold out of our own inventory.

A lot of my training, strategies, and tactics went out the window. No longer was there one colossus dominating our offensive and defensive war plans. Now we had a dozen threats from all over the world, all equally capable of triggering a response from Air Force assets.

The business world has changed in a similar way. There used to be corporate superpowers who locked horns with each other in long-term, siege-type combat. General Motors versus Ford. Merck Pharmaceutical versus Pfizer. American Air Lines versus United. They knew each other well, trained against each other, and followed established rules of engagement in a predictable ground game. Ten yards and a cloud of dust.

At the dawn of the new millennium that whole paradigm has shifted. To be successful, companies today have to be able to deploy rapidly against all challengers big and small, embrace new technology, react globally, and not only cut across traditional lines of business, but create entirely new lines of business.

To understand this phenomenon, look no further than to Amazon.com's success in the face of traditional brick-and-mortar retailing. Who would have thought that hundreds of millions of dollars of book sales could have been drained from the cash registers of Barnes & Noble or Waldenbooks—or any store for that matter—by a bookstore that doesn't even exist! But that's exactly what has happened. The convenience of Internet access has offered an alternative to those long lines at a cash register (and long drives across town), with instant access to over 3 million titles.

But never forget that change is constant and the battlefield is always dynamic. The Soviet Union crumbled; the Air Force adapted to new threats. Amazon.com soared to the forefront, but Barnes & Noble must have a few F–15 jocks in its ranks. Have you ever logged on to barnesandnoble.com?

This is a well-matched battle, no doubt about it.

There you have it. The race is continuous, the change is constant, the story is never finished.

SUMMARY

Wars, and business competitions, are won and lost through individual engagements. And what makes the difference in engagement is proficiency of execution—which side is better trained and better prepared to deal with the dynamic nature of a shifting battlefield.

There's no individual on earth better trained for a three-dimensional, fluid battlefield than a U.S. fighter pilot. His individual training by the Air Force, Navy, or Marines is designed in every physical, intellectual, and administrative way to create an executor who accepts only one outcome—winning. Business people, whose tasks are nearly as numerous and demanding as those of a pilot, can adopt similar training to create a high level of personal achievement. But before they can learn the particular empowerment techniques fighter pilots use, they must understand these three rules of successful engagement:

1. Change is good. And what's more, it's inevitable. Embrace it, welcome it, take energy from it, use it to your advantage.

2. Stay current with technology. Don't resist technological advances, even when they make your current operating procedures obsolete. Your competition won't wait for you to catch up.

3. The threat always changes. An entrenched, perennial foe can suddenly vanish. If all your doctrines revolve around that threat, you're vulnerable to the new, fast-moving enemies that can spring up in its wake. Stay flexible and adaptable, even when the new threats aren't yet on your radar scope.

THE SPEAR:
ORGANIZE FOR EXECUTION

We've seen the similarities between air combat and business combat. You've learned the importance of a gung-ho attitude, and an openness to change. Now, how do you put that attitude into action? How do you organize your assets to execute your mission? And how can Air Force techniques help?

THE MISSION

There's an expression in the fighter pilot community—we call ourselves the *pointy end of the spear*. It's a bit of braggadocio, but there's something to it: We actually believe that our organization, the United States Air Force, is like a spear, and as the first players into the theater of battle we fighter pilots constitute its sharp-edged tip. All of the functions within this vast, geographically dispersed "corporation" of 700,000 "employees" are narrowly aligned behind one thing—our missions. There's no empire-building, no bickering, no politics, just one question to be asked: Is what we're doing serving to make the pilots more successful in their missions? From research and development teams to weapons designers to weathermen, everyone has to answer to the same question: Will what we're doing contribute to the success of the mission?

Sure, that may *sound* like a dangerously narrow focus to have. But remember, no matter what tools or tactics we employ in the combat of business, we have to take the battlefield one customer at a time. There's no magic button we can push to sweep the airspace over Kuwait clean at one stroke. Similarly, there's no magic button that can give one company control of, say, the lodging industry. It's one F–15 against one MiG–29. One combat mission—one customer experience—at a time. The reason for the Air Force's record of success is that it accepts the need to align itself, straight and narrow as a spear, behind each individual mission. Any company can be similarly oriented. In fact, most companies already have the basic assets in place. You simply need to be focused—Air Force style—toward the mission.

How do you accomplish this? We use a defined *command structure* and *organizational structure*. Contrary to what you may believe, the Air Force structure is designed to empower the individual—to make it possible for the individual to excel and accomplish his mission.

COMMAND STRUCTURE:
THE VISION IS NOT THE MISSION

The traditional military command structure, however rigid it may seem, has remained in place for a reason. It provides both an organizing structure and a tried-and-true way for the general vision of a commanding officer to be conveyed, rank by rank, as a set of specific orders that can be given to individual combatants as *missions*.

As a fighter pilot, I care very much about the overall objectives laid out by the general officers of the United States Air Force. In fact, I have to buy into them so totally, so enthusiastically, that I'm willing to risk my life for them. But I don't operate in a generalized world. My world is very specific. I'm an F–15 air superiority fighter pilot. I don't drop bombs. I don't have a thirty-millimeter tank-killing gun like the A–10. I've never even *seen* a tank close up. I do one thing well, and that's provide air cover for ingressing bombers by taking out airborne threats. I do not operate under the same rules as an F–117 Stealth pilot, or an F–16 pilot. My mission objective is very specific, tied totally to my individual capability and my training.

As such, it's imperative that the mission I'm assigned is specific and precise, not vague or general. Imagine if I went up in the air with only the following orders: "Murph, your objective is to kick Saddam Hussein out of Kuwait. Good luck—let's go kick some ass." It's okay for Norman Schwarzkopf to say that; in fact, that's what he's *supposed* to say. His job is to establish an overall objective for the troops, and to do it in such a way that all participants understand it and get behind it. He probably doesn't even know how I do what I do. But he doesn't need to know. He simply needs to lay out a straightforward overall objective that can be divided into manageable parts that, when activated, will lead inexorably to the achievement of his objective.

How does this happen? The military command structure underneath Schwarzkopf has to take his general vision and push it down through the ranks and into the cockpits, subs, and trenches—where it is presented not as a vision, but *as a mission*. Directly underneath Schwarzkopf, the brigadier generals break the vision down into its individual parts—the Army does this, the Air Force does that, and so on. Next, the commanding generals evaluate their individual assets and create an overall operations plan. This is called the *frag*, short for fragmentary order, the overall battle plan broken down into the relevant parts. The bombers, fighters, and ground forces are all commanded to converge on a certain target at a certain time and in a certain sequence.

One level down, other officers convert the frag into even smaller parts. The 1st Fighter Wing and its F–15s do this; the F–117 guys from Holliman do that. The KC–10s will be waiting to give gas here, the A–10s will attack tanks there.

Yet another level down, wing commanders divide the frag again. For example, they might decide that twelve F–15s will be responsible for providing air cover over a specific piece of ground, so that thirty-six bombers can come in under them and pound enemy ground targets that our ground troops will then secure.

With the group objective stated for the F–15s, the individual flight leaders, who might be young captains or lieutenants, will look at the airspace they need to sanitize and organize the F–15s with altitude blocks and lanes of responsibility so that we can absolutely, positively do our job—which is to make certain no one hops on the tails of the bombers.

At this point Schwarzkopf's vision has become a mission for me, the individual pilot. I don't set my sights on something as personally unattainable as kicking Iraqis out of Kuwait, but I am ready to give my life to protect an important lane of airspace with my F–15. I'm ready to give my life in the execution of a *clear, measurable, attainable mission that supports the overall vision of my commander*, with all the details worked out from the moment we leave the briefing room until we all reconvene after the mission, debrief, and then grab a postmission beverage of choice.

How often do companies ask their employees to execute their jobs under the banner of a "mission statement" or a generalized corporate goal? A mission statement is fine, but, like an overall objective, it isn't specific enough to lead anybody anywhere. Mission statements aren't marching orders. They sound good, they make sense, but they have zero effect until the organization breaks them down into finer and finer pieces, from rank to rank, presented clearly to each and every employee as a specific task with a measurable outcome that is his and his alone to perform.

This is the beauty of a command structure. A command structure doesn't exist to codify rank, but rather to help the leader to execute his vision by delegating specific jobs and responsibilities to the appropriate teams. Instead of demeaning people by implying that rank is merely a measure of worth, an organizational hierarchy empowers people by conveying their role in helping the company achieve its objectives. Every person is important to the company and its goals because every person has a job only he can execute. It is both liberating and confidence-building to be given responsibility for a job that is clearly needed for a firm's ultimate success.

And it is exhilarating to have an assignment that you can get your arms around—that you will be successful in executing.

Can you see how this would motivate someone? I know I can sanitize airspace with my jet. I understand why that's important to the F–16s and Wild Weasels who knock out ground targets. They in turn know their success is crucial to the bomber crews coming in behind them. And the B–52 crews know what their bombing runs mean to the soldiers slogging into the theater on the ground.

Watch what happens as all these puzzle pieces start falling into place. Each individual executes a specific mission with an unmistakable goal and a measurable outcome. No one's expecting the bomber pilots to come in and bat cleanup for us fighters, nor are the men on the ground expected to finish up the bombing job. And none of us is going to have to worry about logistics or supplies.

When we go in, it's with the confidence that everyone has an individual part to play—and that if we all succeed, ultimately the mission will succeed as well.

Like the Air Force, your company should use its command structure to filter a general vision down to the level of the individual employee. And it shouldn't be a great leap from the general vision to the individual missions, either. There should be a logical, *sequential* breakdown of the vision, so that each group can responsibly accomplish its human-scale goals. Put simply: The more your employees understand how important their roles are to the company's future, the better they'll be at doing their jobs.

ORGANIZATIONAL STRUCTURE: ALIGNMENT TOWARD THE MISSION

All right. If an organization like the Air Force really does align its assets behind the mission as pointedly as the shaft of a spear, how can your company do the same thing?

The Four Components of the Organization

Two hundred and twenty-five years of experimentation have taught the U.S. military that there are four major components to an effective military mission: *operations, combat support, logistics,* and *communications*. And every company of any size can benefit by treating its assets the same way. Let me break down the role of each component:

1: *Operational Assets*

The first elements of the Air Force to go into battle, operational assets are the forces that open the door for the rest of the action; in your company, they're the front-line employees whose mission it is to close down competition and open the door to new business opportunities. In battle there are two types of operational assets—*air superiority assets* and *air-to-ground assets*—and each has its parallel in the business world.

Air Superiority Assets   When hostilities break out and we're called into action, our air superiority assets—like the F–15—are the first to deploy. In war, we want to achieve air superiority quickly over enemy territory, which means sweeping the skies clear of enemy air-attack assets, and dominating the air over the battlefield. Battlefield commanders must have air superiority. Until he controls the skies, a commander can't bring in troops, water, food, weapons, ammunition, and all the materials he'll need for the conduct of war.

In August 1990, when President Bush put into motion Operation Desert Shield, the 1st Tactical Fighter Wing was the first Air Force wing sent to the Persian Gulf. In one rapid deployment, seventy-two F–15s flew eighteen nonstop hours over the Atlantic Ocean, across Europe, and over the Mediterranean; refueled twelve times; and got on station within seventy-two hours of the initial call-up.

In the business world you have air superiority assets of your own. Who are the first people sent into a territory? Who are the first people to engage your customers? Of course, they're your marketing, sales, and customer service people, either out in the field, on the sales floor, or across a counter. They're the first people to take a new product to the customer, the first to demonstrate a new item in the store, the first to make an overture to a customer. They are your F–15s. They create and maintain clean airspace within which other personnel can perform.

Air-to-Ground Assets   Of course, sales and customer service alone can't win an economic war, just as F–15s alone can't win a shooting war. That's why there's a second asset built into the pointy end of the spear. To be successful in combat, you've got to wear down your opponent, blunt his ability to make war against you, and erode his will to engage you head-on. We call the assets that do this work our *air-to-ground assets*. They come in behind our air superiority assets, and in that clear airspace start to pick apart the competition. We use the F–16 Fighting Falcons and the A–10 Warthogs for that job. Day in and day out they pound away at the enemy, tirelessly wearing them down until we're able to take another step forward toward the overall objective. Those assets drop bombs on critical locations like railroads, transportation facilities, and factories to hamper the enemy's ability to make war.

In the business community, what do you have to consolidate your position? What are the air-to-ground assets you use to pound away at the competition? For many companies, it's their product and product mix. Let me give you an example. Procter & Gamble has one of the best sales forces in the world. Its air superiority assets—salespeople, its F–15s—are renowned in the industry: They get their new products on the shelves and they do it efficiently and effectively. But they don't stop there. The P&G sales force is supported by a very effective fleet of A–10s and F–16s. Once the sales force gets a P&G product on the shelves, P&G brings in the ground pounders and goes after the space next to that product, and the space next to it. Soon the competition has been banished to the back end of the aisle, and the shelves are so packed with P&G products that nearly every option the customer has is a P&G brand. (Next time you're in a supermarket, stop by the laundry-detergent aisle and check out how many powder detergents are made by P&G—it'll astound you.) The territory has been marked, the toehold consolidated. Mission accomplished.

Once the air superiority assets have paved the way, the day-in, day-out air-to-ground pounding begins. New products; new features; product extensions. New sizes, multipacks, jumbo economy packs. By constantly strengthening its presence and position, a company like P&G protects its turf and builds its defenses, keeping the competition off-guard until domination is complete.

2: *Combat Support Assets*

Once you've entered the arena and have secured a toehold, you need to oversee the battlefield, protecting your position from surprise counterattacks and unwanted skirmishes—and in the Air Force what we use for protection are our *combat support assets*, which follow the operational assets behind enemy lines and provide special services in support of the mission.

In the Air Force we have an airplane called the Airborne Warning and Control Center (AWACS).

I'm sure you've seen pictures of this odd-looking aircraft, which carries a big radar dish on its back; its role is to fly right up to the edge of the combat area and look 200 nautical miles in all directions using its powerful radar, monitoring any targets that happen to be airborne. AWACS controllers can tell the F–15 pilots where the enemy is, what direction they're heading, what nationality they are, and probably what they had for breakfast. It is an amazing asset, and gives the United States a huge advantage on the battlefield.

In the business world, what are your early warning assets? Well, most companies don't have an equivalent of the AWACS plane, but they do have a team of employees who could accomplish the same goal—if they were trained to do so. When was the last time your company made a point of encouraging its employees to *listen to the customer?* To *listen to the marketplace?* Management consultants have been preaching this message for years, but it hasn't stuck yet—and that's a mistake. Listening to the customer and watching the marketplace can be as critical to your success as AWACS is to ours. If everybody on your front lines actively listened to the customer—monitored real-life performance in the field, yours *and* the competition's—you'd have a dynamic intelligence network keeping you in touch with every sign of activity in your market area. And your operational assets—your sales and marketing teams—could act swiftly and surely to deal with the new conditions.

A common early warning of a threat against your position is news of a test-marketing effort by your competitor. Test markets are sometimes undertaken with elaborate secrecy, and all the ruses that characterize the military's "black" (top secret) programs. Maybe your competitor has a new formula. Maybe it has a new slogan or a new price point. Whatever product attribute it wants to test, it wants to keep the testing program hidden from its competitors as long as possible. Often test markets will be conducted in geographically isolated areas, a long way from the major markets. The idea is to simulate a national launch, but to do it quietly. If the campaign is successful locally, the manufacturer might roll it out regionally or even nationally. If not, it may work out the bugs and then relaunch.

But it can be difficult for any competitor to maintain that kind of secrecy for long, particularly if you've got your sales force trained to listen, observe, and watch its every move—to be your AWACS. What an advantage it would be to learn about a potential competitive threat while it's still in test, to have time to respond, to blunt it or prepare your own defense. A savvy salesperson who feeds such intelligence back to the home office is priceless. One piece of information can lead to one small but important strategic move—and such a move, whether defensive or offensive, may prevent the kind of major shakeup in the marketplace that can have serious implications for the company.

Active Intelligence Gathering   Not surprisingly, the Air Force puts very strong emphasis on looking—really *looking*—at our competition. We don't just passively listen. There's a second part to keeping an eye on the battlefield. We employ another combat support asset called the *intelligence asset*. We *actively* listen for signs of change. We *actively* look for our threats. And you can, too.

Most people know that the Air Force puts a large proportion of its resources and many of its best minds into the intelligence branches. We're never satisfied with guesswork—at least not when it comes to monitoring enemy activities. To that end, we actively gather intelligence. We even designed and created a special reconnaissance aircraft to help us do the job—the SR–71 Blackbird. It is one of the most sophisticated airplanes ever built. This aircraft flies three to four times the speed of sound at the edge of space—at 70,000 to 80,000 feet. It flies that high to eliminate any surface-to-air missile (SAM) threat, and travels that fast to eliminate any fighter interceptor threat. Its purpose? To spy on our competition! Its very sophisticated cameras are capable of taking incredibly detailed pictures of things on the ground. How detailed? If you were driving your car on I–75, it could take a clear picture of your license plate. If it was a convertible and the top was down, it could see how many miles were on your odometer. This astonishing capability was developed not last year with supercomputers, but in the late 1950s, by engineers using slide rules, pencils, and paper. That's how seriously invested the Air Force was in looking at our competitor, the Soviet Union, during the height of the Cold War.

Who's watching your competition? Maybe back at the home office there's an entire department of people gathering intel for you, and if there is, great. But that would be the exception. As much as modern business has advanced, most companies today still don't place a high priority on competitive intelligence gathering. They think it sounds expensive—but it doesn't have to be. All it takes is people. Who is your most important intelligence agent? You! You can be that high-flying asset that takes pictures of the competition. The only difference between you and the SR–71 is that you probably haven't been asked to do the job. But why not? Actively watching the competition has proven to be one of the most effective activities a company can undertake. Billionaire Sam Walton of Wal-Mart made a weekly habit of it. He would take time from his everyday work and walk through his competitors' stores, noting everything they did right and everything they did wrong. He didn't just rely on his market research department. He didn't wait for passive intelligence to come in from the field. He was his own market research department and reconnaissance asset, overflying the entire United States to know exactly what his many competitors were doing. In fact, he often got in trouble for walking through a competitor's store with a tape recorder, making notes and observations, which angered the store managers so much they would try to confiscate his tapes.

The point is, Sam Walton knew how important it was to watch the competition. And, like him, you should set aside time to monitor them, as part of your regular operations. The Marriott Corporation does this, with what it calls its "I Spy" program. Marriott sends its employees out to spend the night in competitive hotels, and asks those employees to report back on all the variables that can make or break a guest experience—things like the speed of the check-in process, the cleanliness of the rooms, how quickly the front desk answers the phone, and the food service. Other companies employ "mystery shoppers" to shop their competition—and even to shop their own stores as a quality check!

Everyone in the organization can do this sort of aggressive observing and listening. Every company can set up a procedure to give people the time to "mystery shop" the competition and report their observations. Who knows what detail may mean something to the sales analysts back in the home office?

The unexpected intel windfall happens in my business, too. When I land my F–15, before I can even unstrap my shoulder harness and get my helmet off, before my engines have quit turning, an intel representative puts a ladder on the canopy rails, climbs up, and starts drilling me with questions. He even has a little card so he doesn't forget the "mandatory" questions. Let's say I've just spent eight hours in a combat air patrol orbit (CAP). He'll ask me, "Murph, what did you see up there today?" and I'll tell him I saw nothing but blue sky and clouds.

Then he'll ask, "Did you see any contrails?"

Why's he asking about that when I've already told him I saw no sign of enemy activity whatsoever? Because he's not just interested in enemy positions, he's interested in making sure *we* all fly as safely as possible. You see, contrails only form at very specific altitudes and in very specific conditions. When a jet encounters those conditions its exhaust plume crystallizes into ice, and a big white streak is etched across the sky behind it. Contrails create a big, beautiful target for enemy anti-aircraft fire and opposing jets—and it doesn't matter if you're a B–52 or a Stealth fighter, if you hit this layer, you're going to draw a line in the sky. Once we know the altitude where contrails are forming, we can avoid it and protect ourselves against detection. The F–15 drivers in my squadron who come on station after me will appreciate that bit of knowledge, especially if they encounter a threat in the air.

Can you see how a seemingly unimportant detail becomes such a vital intelligence asset? Any employee can make a contribution like that, just by being an active observer—a walking SR–71.

3: *Logistic Assets*

The third asset to be deployed in any given operation is the *logistics asset*. Logistics people don't go behind enemy lines; they keep the front lines supplied.

For every fighter pilot in the sky, there are ten logistics support people on the ground. They're the people who send your paycheck to your spouse so you can concentrate on your mission. They're the people who talk to the manufacturers and get 50 million machine gun rounds shipped out to the Persian Gulf. They're the people who feed, clothe, and water the troops. They're the people who provide the enormous administrative machinery that supports the entire organization.

Clearly, bad logistics can kill a company as surely as the competition. The great Allied advance into the Huertgen Forest in World War II ground to a halt because we couldn't get supplies into the forward areas. Thousands died because the combat drew to a standstill, giving the enemy time to regroup. How often has your product been out of stock on a supermarket shelf? If the logistics system can't keep shelf space full, the sales force might as well stay home. Logistics has to be sharply aligned behind the pointy end of the spear. Can you imagine running out of meat at a McDonald's restaurant, or out of sheets at a Fairfield Inn? Of course not. It's unthinkable. Extraordinary logistical support can be a tremendous competitive advantage—witness the tremendous distribution system of NAPA Auto Parts, among other examples. Poor logistics, on the other hand, can mean death.

Not long ago we were conducting a seminar for Wal-Mart. During a break, one of the bright young executives came up to me and told me how important good logistics are to store profits. It seems Wal-Mart, like all mass retailers, has to maintain a precarious balance between keeping store shelves fully stocked, on one hand, and building up excessive inventory on the other. Considering that Wal-Mart carries tens of thousands of items and has hundreds of stores across the nation, I could see how important this could be. The solution for Wal-Mart, in simple terms, was to integrate all its digital technologies so that even as a tube of Crest was being checked out of a store in Tulsa, a command was being sent to its warehouse in Bentonville to load more Crest onto the next truck bound for Tulsa. Moreover, each truck has a global positioning system receiver so the transportation department can track its movement. If a truck breaks down, the transportation department knows about it electronically before it gets the call from the roadside—and a backup truck is already in motion.

Now that's logistics at its best!

4:   *Communications*

The fourth asset that we align in the spear is *communications*. This is the connecting link between operations, combat support, and logistics, and the arterial system that keeps vital information flowing like lifeblood throughout the body.

I recently traveled with a salesperson for a large sporting goods company. We were going from Oklahoma to Texas. He had an appointment with the tennis professional at a large resort. The pro was a very busy man, but he wanted the latest products in his shop because a good portion of his annual income came from shop sales. So, unlike a lot of teaching pros, he really worked with the sales reps to find out about new products and find the right inventory mix.

The salesman was running half an hour late. His previous appointment had gone long, the traffic was bad, and we were on a stretch of interstate without many stops. Tennis pros book their lives in half-hour increments. I looked out the window and counted the cell phone towers. "When are you going to call him?" I asked my companion.

"As soon as I see a gas station," he answered. I watched more cell towers pass. His company obviously thought cell phones were a luxury. By the time he stopped at a gas station to call, his appointment had been canceled. Lack of communications basics cost the man a good sale.

Communication may have been the key to winning Operation Desert Storm and Desert Shield. The coalition forces aligned against Iraq consisted of Americans, Brits,

Canadians, French, Saudis, Kuwaitis, and more, each bringing their own equipment, their own tactics, and their own
disparate languages to the table. To win, it was vital that we
all get on the same page, and coordinate our capabilities and
timing. Real-time telephone, video, and teleconference communications made that possible. Moreover, with satellite
communications capability, squadron commanders in the battlefield could contact manufacturers in the United States for
help with equipment problems. Global Positioning Satellites
could schedule deliveries to their men day or night, simply by
using accurate coordinates. We truly became digital warriors
in 1991—and look at the results.

Today, news moves quickly. Information is power. Time is
of the essence. If real-time communication hasn't become a
priority in your company, make it one today. There are simply
too many tools available to enhance communication: Cell
phones. Voice mail. Digital pagers. The Internet. Intranets.
E-mail. The World Wide Web.

But just as important as having the means and training to
use modern communications systems is having the infrastruc-
ture to move the communication to the right parties. The
military excels at this. We can deliver real-time satellite
imagery to a battlefield commander with studio-quality tele-
com systems. In fact, the Internet itself, originally known as
ARPAnet, was developed by the U.S. military to provide us
with an alternate communications pathway in the event that a
nuclear war or an electromagnetic pulse bomb took out our
conventional communications circuits.

One of the most effective communications systems around
is an *intranet*—an in-house online network designed to help
information be shared throughout a company. If you haven't
built a corporate intranet yet, don't wait any longer. I recently
saw one brilliant system in place at a certain book publisher's
sales force. This company has equipped its sales, marketing,
and management people with laptop computers and
modems—and built into the laptop is its corporate intranet,

which features real-time sales data and a company-wide bulletin board. A salesperson in one state can post a message about a hot-moving book in his territory; that message can be read by another salesperson in another state, signaling him to recommend increasing orders at a store moments before he walks in to make his call. Back at the home office, the vice president of marketing, the company president, and the head of distribution can also read the postings and make adjustments to their plans. It is like a twenty-four-hour sales meeting, with ideas flying back and forth, up and down the organization, all designed to maximize the power of the company's air superiority asset—the salesperson.

SUMMARY

The Air Force is organized to deploy its assets like the simplest of combat weapons—a spear. The pointy end—the combat pilots—are backed up by a long and tightly focused structure that exists solely to aid the successful execution of individual missions. A time-honored structural hierarchy exists to transform the organization's general objectives into specific, individual missions, and those missions can be assigned to the proper individuals as the orders travel down through the ranks.

Further, it has organized itself into basic units—operations, combat support, logistics and communications—that comprise the full scope of the organization's capabilities, and that have their analogs in the business world:

Operations: In the Air Force these are the front-line pilots, in business the sales and marketing teams.

Combat support: In the Air Force these are intelligence assets and specialty aircraft that support and enhance the performance of the front-liners. In the business world a company can mimic this strategy with a wide range of support activities—from encouraging employees to watch the marketplace, to mystery shopping the competition, to keeping its product line innovative, varied, and dominant.

Logistics: For Air Force and civilian employees alike, logistics refers to the administration of combat, and logistical efficiency has an impact on every aspect of the organization. Personnel, payroll, shipping, inventory, purchasing—not the glamour jobs, but vital to the accomplishment of our mission objectives.

Communications: The information link between all units of the organization. Information not shared or transmitted is information wasted. Communication is the backbone of the mutual-support model that has made the Air Force one of the most successful organizations on earth, and most successful companies can chalk up at least part of their success to concerted in-house networking.

When the Air Force embarks on any new mission, then, it has every asset it needs in place, ready to contribute to the common goal of victory. With a little careful attention to organization and support, your company can be just as successful.

THE VALUE OF INTELLIGENCE

When I fly, I want to be the smartest sonofabitch in the sky. I want to know who I'm up against, what they're flying, where they are, what they're carrying, and what the ground threats are. I want to know everything, I want it right, and I want a minimum of surprises. Nobody in my group is launching unless we've received a critical mass of intel. We've talked about intelligence assets already, but what I'm talking about now isn't moment-by-moment AWACS updates but *primary* intelligence—the background information that I take into consideration when I'm planning my mission. This intel is so important that I won't—*I can't*—plan a mission without it.

There's a second component to it, though, and you probably haven't heard of it. Intelligence briefings will get me off the ground, but *situational awareness* keeps me alive in the air. Situational awareness is not found in a manual or a top secret report, but every fighter pilot has it. Situational awareness can't be built into an aircraft, but everyone uses it. Situational awareness is the God-given ability to make critical, timely observations; to anticipate the opponent's next move; to think three steps ahead; to make adjustments; to update the situation in the cockpit on a second-by-second basis. Situational awareness is the ability to be here-and-now, and project into the future, without forgetting where you're going.

Together, intelligence and situational awareness create a powerful one-two punch. They establish the baseline on which all good mission planning rests, and they come to your rescue when things start to get out of hand. In the coming chapters, you're going to see how fighter pilots plan, execute, and debrief a mission. You're going to see how businesses can adopt the procedures for better sales meetings or smarter customer service. But first things first—and the first thing any fighter pilot needs to accomplish a mission is that combination of intelligence and situational awareness.

CUSTOMIZE YOUR INTELLIGENCE

Do you remember what a SAM is? It's a surface-to-air missile, and it's my worst nightmare. Its purpose is to knock me out of the sky. It's a bad thing to see a SAM, so bad that we always ask the satellite imagery folks or airborne recon to look down and take pictures of their sites before we do anything. Intel then gives me a map with the sites shown as circles, with the size of the circle indicating that site's effective missile range.

We have several support assets to knock them out before they can threaten a guy like me. The F–4G Wild Weasel (now decommissioned), the F–16, and the F/A–18 all have SAM-killing capability. If you're going to downtown Baghdad tomorrow, you'll want these guys on your wing. These assets usually fly a few minutes ahead of the package of inbound aircraft. When the enemy's early warning assets detect these incoming jets, the SAM sites turn on their radars and start sweeping the sky. That's just what our guys are waiting for. As soon as they detect an enemy radar lock on, they fire a radar-seeking HARM missile (high-speed anti-radiation missile) right back down the radar beam. The explosion is, shall we say, devastating, and it's always on the money.

It took the Iraqis a while to figure out what was going on, and we blew up most of their SAM sites before they did. But nothing is ever perfect, and the SAM threat never went totally away, especially with the mobile sites. Pilots still needed up-to-the-minute intelligence before they launched their missions. Moreover, they need *customized* intelligence. Remember, I don't drop bombs. I don't need to know anything about lasing conditions over the target area (like a low cloud deck, something an F–117 driver needs to know about). I'm flying at 30,000 feet. I need to know about enemy fighters, contrail levels, high-altitude SAM sites. I need intelligence customized to my mission.

Remember the guy who ran up to my cockpit with his list of questions even as my engines were winding down? He's part of a vast system designed to gather information, organize it, and redistribute it to the right people in a timely fashion. What he learns from pilots like me is merged with similar reports from a hundred other pilots, with SR–71 photos, satellite imagery, battlefield reports, reconnaissance flights—anything and everything that might keep us alive, help us execute our missions, and help achieve the overall objective of the organization.

Before we fly our next mission, this same person is there to brief us on the threats, the current situation in the air, and all sorts of seemingly minor but important details from the collected intelligence of the previous few hours.

The purpose of intelligence gathering, analysis, and dissemination is to provide specific help to the people who have to execute the missions. Intelligence gathering is driven by the needs of the users. To be effective, it has to be customized. Business intelligence is no different; it needs to be customized for its end users. Each operational asset has a different information need. The national sales manager requires intelligence data that wouldn't be useful to the emerging-markets sales division. The OEM reps need different intel from the direct sales department. The people in the paint department need different information from those selling lawn and garden products. Good, useful intelligence has to be customized.

As I said earlier, if I've observed any universal weakness in the course of meeting with thousands of business executives, it is that intelligence gathering resources of most companies are almost nonexistent.

What a pity. Can you imagine how powerful members of a sales force would be if they had a complete rundown of competitive activity, new promotions, new pricing plans, test market activities, and all the possible objections they'd have to overcome before they

go out on a three-day sales trip? Can you imagine briefing the customer service department in the morning with a rundown of all
the "specials" and promotions announced by the competition for
the coming weekend? Not only does everyone perform better, look
better, and do more for the customers, but they save themselves
needless worry and wasted motion.

That's the purpose of the basic intel brief. It lays out the underlying information that people need to execute their immediate
mission.

Where is your intelligence department? Why not institute
weekly briefings for your salespeople? If you're trying to come up
with reasons that you can't—*we're too busy; it's too difficult; it would
cost too much*—don't bother. Penny-pinching never won a battle.

SITUATIONAL AWARENESS

There's a second component to intelligence, and that's *situational
awareness*—SA for short. Let me tell you what it means. SA is a
state of mind, a level of awareness that's almost superhuman. For a
fighter pilot, having good SA means that while you're in a nine-G
turn with three bandits on your tail, a 10,000-foot mountain ridge
to your left, a SAM site ten miles to the north, and an inbound
package due in twenty seconds, you see it all in the past, present,
and future. You know where you've been. You know where you are.
You know where you're going. You know your fuel state and
weapons status. You see where the three bandits are headed, you
know their weapons engagement zones (WEZ), and you intu-
itively sense their plan. You visualize where the package is in rela-
tion to the bandits. You sense the mountain range and the SAM
site and you integrate it all without thinking about it consciously.

That is high SA. It's the kind of intelligence brilliant detectives
have—the same ability that lets them walk into a crime scene and
see things an ordinary person would never notice.

What does SA have to do with the intelligence process? *SA is
the real-time version of intelligence.* Good intel lays out the basic sit-

uation and has you prepared for the mission, for that sales call or planning meeting. High SA enables you to update the situation at precisely the moment you need to apply it—*in the present*. If you have it, it can give you incredible power.

Consider the moment you walk into your customer's corporate headquarters. You know where you've been, where you are, where you're going. You're briefed. You have a good head for your product and competitive activity. You're about to make a presentation. Now's your chance to update yourself, to let your SA kick in. Is there anything you can observe—*right now*—that contradicts what you've been assuming to be true? Is there anything that invalidates any part of your presentation? Do you notice anything that would make your presentation more salient or memorable? Any problem that you or your product can help solve? If it's a retail environment, did you notice long lines at the cash register? Were there people stocking shelves, or were the shelves in disarray? Has the competition installed a new floor display that wasn't on your intel briefing?

SA can be useful in service positions, too. Let's say you're in the paint department at Home Depot and a customer approaches you with a can of flat latex. There's nothing he can ask you about the product that you can't answer. But do you observe his appearance, the way he holds the product, his body language? Do you sense how many other people are approaching with a question or a complaint? Is there a backup at the paint shaker or the tinting area? Have you figured out how you're going to manage the logjams? Where is your nearest assistant? How busy is everyone else today?

If you're a manager on the floor, are you observing the weather, the number of cars in the parking lot, the demeanor of customers in the store, the level of customer interest in your specials or new displays, and the overall situation in the store? Are you taking in this minute-to-minute intelligence, anticipating problems or opportunities that will arise five minutes from now?

Pilots who develop high SA are invariably the aces of the base. They're invariably the ones chosen to command. SA empowers them. They are so far ahead of the rest of us that they usually shoot us down before we have a full picture of the engagement.

You know who they are in business, too. Some people call them *high-bandwidth individuals*, people who seem to be quick on the uptake, who know what you're about to say even as you start a sentence. They are observant people. They want to see everything. Bill Gates is legendary for integrating complex issues that cut across a multiplicity of disciplines. *He* has high SA.

But don't worry if you don't feel you're the most intuitive person in the world: SA can be practiced, developed, and applied just like any other discipline. You can train to heighten your own SA. Do dry runs as you enter a department store: Scan the activities around you. See how much you really see when you're thinking SA. We pilots do a lot of "chair flying": We practice a mission with imaginary radio calls, imaginary bandits, imaginary refueling. We "fly" the mission in our chairs and "see" our three-dimensional environment the way we see it in the cockpit. Professional athletes have good SA; they, too, often play games through in their heads before they actually go on the basketball court or the football field or walk down to center court. Once the game begins they can sense the flow of the game, anticipate what the other team is going to do, and see everyone on both teams in a kind of slow motion. Magic Johnson, for example, had an uncanny knack for sensing where his teammates were going to be, and could zing the basketball right to them, whether he was looking at them or not. Laker players always knew to be alert when Magic had the ball; if they weren't paying attention, Magic's no-look pass would smack them in the forehead.

SA is like your own on-board intel system. There are many ways to develop it, but first of all you've got to know it's there.

ENVIRONMENTAL FACTORS

There is a third and final variable in the intelligence equation— what we call *environmental factors*. When something seems obvious, people often forget to communicate it to others—and that can be a big mistake. Let me give you an example.

Not long ago I had a tough mission. Brief, start, check-in, and takeoff went as planned. My four-ship of F–15s screamed into the air in good shape, and then we were in perfect line-abreast formation at 30,000 feet, approaching our CAP point. It was time to check in with the eye in the sky—our AWACS controller.

"Bandsaw, Fang One One checking in at 30,000 feet." Bandsaw is the AWACS. "Bandsaw, authenticate, Alpha Charlie."

The voice on the radio came back: "X-Ray."

With that, I knew for sure that this was, indeed, my AWACS controller, and not an Iraqi pilot vectoring me into a SAM site. If he hadn't said "X-Ray," I would not have talked to him.

This radio verification is one part of the elaborate security measures we take in the Air Force. Every pilot carries on his knee board a verification card on which are printed horizontal and vertical lines of letters. These are authentication codes and they change frequently, twenty-four hours a day.

After the authentication I'd say, "Fang One One is checking in at flight level 300. Fang One One has thirty-two minutes of play time. Fang One One is loaded four-by-four-by gun." Translation: There are four of us at 30,000 feet, carrying a certain type of weapon, with about half an hour's worth of fuel left.

Then I'd say, "Are you ready to copy the environment check?" and here's where we communicate what's obvious to us—but not necessarily to anyone else.

There are eighteen technicians in the AWACS. They have thousands of square feet of instruments, radars, and computers at their fingertips. But there's not a window in the whole plane except up in the cockpit—and even if there were, they're hundreds of miles away from me. They need to know from me what the day is like outside— where the sun is, and where the cloud deck is. Why do they need to know? Because if they're going to help me vector in on the enemy, I want them to direct me so that the sun is at my back. I want the enemy to be blinded by the sun, to be flying into it if possible. And if there's a cloud deck below me, I want to be sure I'm above the enemy and not below him, where he could see my jet nicely silhouetted against the dark clouds. I always want to use the environment to my advantage. Their powerful radar, GPS positioning data, and other cosmic devices are useful, but they need real-time intel from me and my eyeballs to complete the tactical picture.

That radio interchange integrates my data with their data and adds the finishing touches by painting a picture of the environment. That final piece of information—stuff that's obvious to me in the cockpit—gives the intelligence people on the AWACS the final piece in the puzzle. Now, when they feed vectors back to me, they'll have been computed with every contingency in mind.

So, how does that apply to business? Think about it. The home office is 2,000 miles away. The people there see reports and data streams, but they wouldn't know what your buyer looked like if he walked in front of them. They have no idea what sort of visual impact the competition's strategies have inside different kinds of stores. They can't see it, because they aren't there—*but you are*. The environment report I make to an AWACS should be the model for an important part of your intel feedback from your sales call. If you want others to help you, the more they know, the better.

I've also seen this kind of environmental-factor report be useful in my post–Air Force flying days. Believe it or not, each and every airplane in the United Airlines fleet is a mini-AWACS plane; we help each other by passing our environment reports up and down the line. I remember a trip not too long ago. I was flying copilot on a new Boeing 767. Passengers love the 767, in part because of its reputation for having one of the smoothest rides in the air. We pilots like to think we also have something to do with that—and on United there's a double chance that we do. On this particular trip, as we went cross-country, another United flight twenty minutes ahead of us passed real-time intelligence back to my plane. It warned us about a patch of clear air turbulence at 33,000 feet— easy enough to avoid, but this gave us a heads-up. We requested an altitude change to 31,000 feet, and our customers got what they wanted—a nice smooth ride. And United came out the winner.

In a time when information is almost more valuable than the dollar itself, every company should make sure its intelligence channels are fast and efficient—and that its employees understand the importance of both intelligence and awareness. Alertness—to your environment, your needs, and the needs of your colleagues—is one of the keys to success.

THE INTEL VAULT

Thanks to movies like *Top Gun*, everyone believes that the life of a fighter pilot is a life of action and adventure. I won't deny that there are plenty of high-action moments in a fighter pilot's life, but there are dozens of "thinking" hours for every hour of flying time. We don't hop in the jet until a whole lot of mental work and planning is done. A huge part of our preparation for air combat is the gathering of intelligence, analyzing that intelligence, and creating a mission plan that takes advantage of what we've learned. Intel gathering in the military, especially for a fighter pilot, is a full-time job. We always keep our eyes and ears open, both for intelligence/technology leaks within our own group and for intelligence about threats coming in from the outside.

Unknown factors make us nervous. We train for contingencies and unexpected events, but we don't want a steady diet of them. With so much at stake (the mission, the battle, the war, our *lives*), it pays to know as much as possible about the threat. As a flight lead, I want to know what kinds of planes I might be facing, and from what direction. I want to know how many of them there are; where they refuel; whether they have mid-air refueling capability; where their pilots were trained, and how long ago; what weapons they carry; their known radio frequencies; any code signals that we know about; how they fly in formation; what dogfight tendencies they have; whether they can see at night; and what tactics have worked successfully to defeat them in the past. I want the full scouting report, just as if I were the coach of a football team going into the Super Bowl. That competitive information is a critical component to all my combat mission plans.

Can you imagine the Air Force launching a package of airplanes that don't know exactly where they're going and precisely when they're going to get there? Or who might show up to fight them? And what kind of weapons they have? There are far too many product launches that fail because the timing wasn't right, or because a competitor launched a countercampaign with a superior product. There are far too many nationwide sales promotions that fall flat because the company failed to anticipate the moves of the competition.

Business people all acknowledge that they need a better intelligence capability. They struggle with how to create it. Lately, many have hit upon the notion that hiring former CIA agents to spy for them will give them an advantage. Well, that sounds effective, but for most companies that level of commitment shouldn't be necessary, or advisable, until something else happens first: making everybody in the company an intelligence gatherer. You say you're not trained to be a spy? Neither am I! I fly airplanes. But I am trained to observe, and I dutifully report my observations to someone who can draw important conclusions from what I tell him. All it takes is eyes and ears.

Nearly everyone in your company interacts with the customer at some time, and observes the competition from time to time, especially in a retail environment. Just as I inform AWACS of the environment in my flying area, anyone can observe and report real-time environmental intelligence to a fellow employee who can put that information to good use. Any smart company will make a point of this to its employees: They don't call it *intelligence* for nothing.

SUMMARY

The gathering of intelligence on the environment and on the competition isn't someone else's job. It's *your* job. Whether you're Sam Walton or a floor supervisor who sneaks into the competition every couple of weeks for surveillance, staying alert and collecting information is an important part of your contribution—your *oblig-ation*—to your company. Time and time again, a single employee's casual observation can lead to the kind of far-reaching, important change that gives your company an advantage on the business battlefield. And conveying that message to your employees can be a vital first step in creating an effective combat mission plan—the blueprint for action we'll create in the next chapter.

THE SIX STEPS TO
COMBAT MISSION PLANNING

Out there on the runway, shimmering in the noonday heat, a package of twelve aircraft is about to launch into a mission as part of a composite strike force. Four of those aircraft are Air Force F–15s, tasked with a prestrike sweep and escort. Eight are Air National Guard F–16s for the air-to-ground attack. Once airborne they will be joined by two Navy EA6-B radar jammers coming off a nearby aircraft carrier and two KC–10 refueling tankers that will orbit on a refueling track positioned at the mission's mid-point.

Like all modern-day strike packages, this force is a diverse group. It incorporates different aircraft with different airspeeds, and all have different responsibilities. As often now happens, they're even starting the strike from different places and from different branches of the military. Despite that, they all know exactly what they're supposed to do. They know the call signs, the altitude restrictions, all of the time hacks, where to position themselves, what the others are doing, and when to execute their respective responsibilities. The whole package has been orchestrated down to the smallest operational detail. The mission will go so smoothly, you'd think the pilots had flown together for years.

In fact, they've probably never met.

A strike package has a lot in common with a business. It isn't all that different from a major sales presentation, a new business pitch, a brand review, or even an annual shareholders' meeting. In both cases, diverse assets are being brought together to achieve the overall objective of the mission. A mix of people and departments, each with specific roles, is readied for the mission, and invested with a we-won't-lose attitude. And the crux of the whole thing is always *planning*.

Except that you and I do it differently.

As we discussed in the previous chapter, the first step to planning is intelligence gathering. Then, once you've got as much accurate, up-to-the-minute intelligence as you can gather, it's time to create the plan. In business, it's usually called a *business plan*. In my world, it's called a *combat mission plan*.

COMBAT MISSION PLANNING

No one plans missions better than the United States Air Force. As I've said before, it's a necessity. Air combat is so fluid, so fast-breaking, so ever-changing that even the variables are dynamic. To fight and win in this environment takes a masterful synthesis of outside intelligence, complete knowledge of internal capabilities, and a plan that matches up those capabilities one-on-one with the opponent's weak spots.

"Plan" is the key word here. I can't tell you how many times I've stood in front of my jet at an air show and listened to an enthusiastic father tell his wide-eyed son how much fun we pilots must have "just flying around up there looking for the bad guys." Well, I'm here to tell you, fighter pilots don't spend any time "just flying around"—and especially not if there's any threat involved. Every mission we undertake, every hour of flying time we log, is planned—whether we're engaging an enemy or simply flying from one U.S. base to the next. Planned, and planned *meticulously*—down to the last flipped control-panel switch.

Over the last few years, we at Afterburner Seminars have distilled the complex mission planning process used by the United States Air Force into something we call the Six Steps to Combat Mission Planning. This is a logical, step-by-step process you can use to learn how to think about your mission, and how to marshal every resource of your organization toward its success. We've guided dozens of companies through this process, and seen it successfully applied by PC manufacturers, retailers, hotel chains, phone companies, accounting firms, pharmaceutical companies, life insurance companies, and packaged goods manufacturers—as well as by leaning-forward individuals from department heads to front-line customer service representatives to entrepreneurs. They have found, as we have, that following these steps can propel any organization into higher realms of efficiency, accountability, and personal performance.

STEP ONE: DEFINE THE MISSION OBJECTIVE AND PUT IT INTO A CONCISE STATEMENT

A mission objective is the clear, measurable, tactical statement of a goal that can be achieved by those people responsible for its execution.

The first step in any plan is to formulate a clear mission objective. Again, I'm not talking about the kind of big-picture strategic objective laid out by General Schwarzkopf in the Persian Gulf. I'm talking about a *mission* objective—a tactical statement that tells *me* (not the B–52 bomber pilot) exactly *what* I am going to do, *where* I'm going to do it, and *when* I'm going to do it. Here's a breakdown of all the requirements of a successful mission statement:

A. It must be absolutely clear and understandable. There's no room for ambiguity in a mission objective. Specificity is the goal here. The more specific the objective, the more linear everyone's thinking becomes. What you're after is a hard, straight line from the objective to the desired action, not a wavy, fuzzy line. How do you know when it's specific enough? When the objective is so clear that *it cannot be broken down any further*, you're there.

B. It must be measurable. You must include an outcome that is quantifiable. Why is this important? So you know precisely how to measure success or failure, before, during, and after the mission.

The goal is 100 percent effectiveness; if you fall short of complete success, you'll want to know why, by how much, and in what respect. If you can figure out that much, a remedy shouldn't be too far behind. And if your mission *isn't* laid out in simple black and white, you'll never be able to discern what you did right and what you did wrong. A team that can't learn from its mistakes is bound to repeat them, and from a fighter pilot's perspective, blind repetition is a sure way to get pilots killed.

Many companies eliminate this characteristic in their plans. They either fail to specify a clear goal, or they set the goal in such broad terms that success or failure is impossible to judge. In so doing, they eliminate the possibility of systematic, institutional improvement—and that's a crucial component to long-term combat superiority.

C. *It must be achievable.* This doesn't mean your goals should be easy. It simply means what it says—that they must be achievable. As fighter pilots, we know what we *can* do and what we *cannot* do. As I've said before, F–15 pilots don't drop bombs; if orders ever came down that we were to strap on a bunch of bombs and go after some ground target, we'd be forced to come to one of two conclusions: Either our leaders have no clue what we do, or they don't care if we live or die. Either way, we'd have a disaster on our hands.

Maybe it's happened to you in the business world: You've been given an impossible mission; you've discovered that for some reason you can't seem to communicate with your supervisor; you become wary, demoralized, and reluctant to begin in the first place. You become depressed, disenfranchised with your management and ultimately your company. Misjudged or unclear missions can be fatal to a company's continuing health. Those conceiving the plans have a responsibility to know whom they're talking to, and what they're asking for.

D. *It must support the overall objectives of the organization.* A mission always involves risk. During mine, I could be shot down. During yours, you could lose an important business opportunity. So it's crucial that a mission statement be demonstrably important to the overall campaign—because, in short, your team won't fight hard enough if they're not sure what they're fighting for. In fact, in the Air Force we're taught to challenge an objective that seems to be fraught with obvious risks or is needlessly off target from the general vision. It's not a form of mutiny or disrespect, but rather a means of making sure everyone is on board. As long as we can see a clear link between our mission and the overall objective, there's no reason for debate. We get into our jets and light up the afterburners. The same holds true in business. No one wants to waste time, energy, or resources on a mission that seems to fly wide of the target.

Putting It All Together into a Concise Statement

Let's suppose our commander declares that our fighter wing's mission objective today is "to take out the enemy's communications capability." That's a good mission statement, isn't it? It states our goal clearly. It has a measurable outcome. It can be accomplished with our F–16s, so it is achievable. It even supports the overall vision.

But is it really? Not at all. There are so many components to a communications system—the point of origination, the hard-wire towers, the relay stations, the transmitters, the studios. What are the F–16s really supposed to attack? *When* do they hit it? And what does "take out" mean? You can't measure that.

A better mission objective would be this: "The C3i (Command, Control, Communication, and Intelligence) building in Baghdad will be struck with two 2,000-pound smart bombs at 0300 ZULU tomorrow, by two F–117 Nighthawks." Is that a clear mission objective? Crystal clear. Is it measurable? Absolutely—either they hit the building or they don't. Is it achievable? Yes, the F–117 is designed to deliver smart bombs, and the margin of error for a smart bomb is tiny; hitting a building is not a problem. Does it support the overall vision of the organization? Yes—disabling the enemy's communications will put its entire military structure in disarray, decreasing its capabilities and probably shortening the duration of the war. Can it be broken down any further? No. One building, two bombs. It's gone.

For the F–117 pilots, this a difficult, dangerous mission—*but it is a tremendously empowering mission objective.* It is well within the aircraft's capabilities, well within the pilots' training, and consistent with the overall vision. These pilots will have a very tough flight, but they'll take off because they know they have the ability to execute the mission and can probably get back alive. *Put me in, coach—I'm ready to play.*

Now apply these rules to your company. Your mission objective must have these same four characteristics—clarity, measurability, achievability, and a clear relationship to the company's overall objective. Once put into words and delivered to the appropriate group, it is so specific that it leaves no room for error. And there's no greater motivating force than the posing of a challenge everyone's prepared to meet.

Here are some clear, measurable mission objectives:

"In the present fiscal year, we will increase market share in the canned pineapple category by 12 percent."

"We will reduce overall out-of-stocks in the next twelve months by 37 percent."

"We will sell 5,000 gallons of paint in the greater Greenville area by year-end."

This specificity, this setting of achievable goals—*demanding*, yet still achievable—inevitably leads to huge leaps in efficiency, morale, and enthusiasm. Everyone holding that statement in his hands is suddenly invested in the success of the mission. Everyone realizes that his results will be measured and noticed—and believe it, people want to succeed!

STEP TWO: IDENTIFY THE THREAT

Once you have a clear mission objective, you have to analyze thoroughly the competitive threats to your outcome.

Know your enemy—it's a vitally important concept to a fighter pilot. When someone is trying to kill you, I guarantee that you'll want to know everything there is to know about that adversary. It's also vitally important to you in business. What competitive attributes can hurt your sales? *To know—and articulate—any and all competitive threats to your success: That is the second part of the combat mission plan.*

Primary Threats

The F–15 has a lot of capabilities, but its primary job is to meet and defeat any enemy fighter that comes up to attack. While there are a dozen credible fighters in the world, I'm most likely to engage a MiG–29. This is my primary threat to my mission, my competition. Someday, somewhere, the two of us will be converging in the sky at a closure rate in the thousands of miles per hour—merging *beak to beak,* as we call it—and we're going to dogfight.

Because I want to survive, you can be sure that I know everything there is to know about the MiG—its performance capabilities, its service ceiling, its top speed, its weapons systems. But that's not enough to win. Before I execute my specific mission objective, I'd really like to know what's in the heart and in the gut of the man or woman flying that jet. Before I plant the flag and start turning and burning, I want to know whether he relishes a fight, or prefers to tease and flee. Will he follow typical Russian dogfight protocol, or was he trained by the Pakistanis, who are tenacious dogfighters? Is he likely to be a combat veteran or a brand-new pilot?

During the Persian Gulf War, we respected the skill of the Iraqi pilots; they're good dogfighters. But we also knew that they hadn't been trained to our level of competency. They had a dozen good ways to kill me, but our training gave us some extra skills that they didn't have. Low-level flight, for one. I can engage a MiG at 100 feet or 30,000 feet. It's all the same to me, but the Iraqis hate low-level engagements.

Just as important, we knew their aviation skills were rusty because their training schedule had been sporadic and inconsistent (they were low on aviation fuels and parts), and we also had reason to believe that their morale was generally terrible. Our conclusion: Iraqi pilots probably weren't terribly motivated to get airborne. Our predictions were that if they saw an F–15, or even knew one was nearby, they'd run. If they stuck around and tried to turn with us, there was a good chance they might be on a suicide mission and would be flying by emotion, not by skill—a dangerous situation.

That's how well we got to know our primary threat—we knew not only their equipment but their training, their morale, their likely behavior and the potential risks it entailed. Armed with that knowledge, and confident in our own training and equipment, the pilots of the U.S. Air Force were willing to bet their lives that if they merged beak to beak with an Iraqi MiG, they would engage and they would win.

Do you know your primary competitive threats as well as an F–15 fighter plot knows that MiG? It's vitally important that you do. Products compete with products. Services compete with services. To achieve your mission objective, you must know the competition as well as I know a MiG and its driver.

When I was in the paint business, I made sure my regional sales reps knew the competition firsthand. We held what I called *scrapyard PK (product knowledge) classes*: I made them go to the local scrapyard and pick through the trash, gathering all sorts of things—old doors, rusty metal pipes, siding, and anything else someone might have a reason to paint. They'd take this junk home, lay it out in their backyard, and we'd paint it—half with our paint, half with our competitor's paint. It wasn't easy. It took time. On those hot, humid days in Plano, Texas, we sweated a whole lot. But in the end, my rep learned—*really learned*—about our competitor's products. He learned firsthand why our paint was better than the competition. He saw the competitive brand clog in the sprayer or flow poorly across metal. He felt the paint spread. He knew his enemy. And when he went to see his first buyer he blew the competition away.

Look for the *Hidden* Threats to Your Mission Objective

Believe me, there's more than one threat standing between you and a successful mission. The MiG is my obvious obstacle, just as a competitor's product is yours, but any number of other problems can stop you dead in your tracks.

A particularly devilish one that I face is a specialized SAM called an SA–6. We've talked about SAMs before, but this one is unique—it's specifically designed to reach up into the sky and bring down a high-flying F–15 like me. It can actually outclimb my F–15 in a race, and pull more G's in a turn. So while I'm worrying about my primary threat, I'm also keeping an eye out for SA–6s. The last thing I want to do is to engage an enemy MiG near an SA–6 site.

Unfortunately, that's not the end of my worries. There's AAA—anti-aircraft artillery fire. When AAA batteries spot someone like me, they saturate an area of the sky with shells. We call it *barrage fire*—it's what you saw on CNN in the skies over Baghdad. We plot the AAA sites on our map along with the SAMs. Then there are specialized MiG bases that are tied directly to GCI (ground controlled intercept) radar, a radar system that warns the enemy of an ongoing invasion and radar-vectors MiGs directly onto my tail. You can bet we plot those sites carefully, too.

Together, all of these hidden threats form what we call IADs—integrated air defense systems. When our maps of the enemy IADs are completed, there are hundreds of rings all over the country in question. Iraq, for example, had one of the most intricate and developed IADs in the world. It had layer after layer of very formidable threats. Looking at those intel maps during the pre-flight briefs must have made the pilots think there wasn't a square inch of unprotected land in Iraq. But isn't half the battle knowing what and where the threats are? Of course it is. Once you know your threats, you can take steps to eliminate them.

What are *your* hidden threats? Have you ever plotted the IADs you face? I will guarantee you this—there are more hidden threats to your competitive success than you can possibly imagine. Are there government regulations to which you have to pay special attention? OSHA regs? Do your competition's products meet a higher quality standard than your own? Not long ago, I met the president of a company that manufactures radios for motorcycles and snowmobiles. He has a wonderful product and a solid position in the marketplace, but to strengthen that position, to block competition, he consistently puts his company through ISO 9000 Quality evaluations and consistently scores at the top of his category. His competitors now have to match that level of effort just to compete.

What about your trade policies and terms? Those are some of the most insidious of the hidden threats to your objective. Are you offering better or worse credit terms than your competition? Do you deliver on time? Do you have unrealistically high minimum ordering quantities? Is your product competitive? As we discussed earlier, every department of your organization and every policy of your company has to be aligned—*like a spear*—behind the objective of your sales or service mission. Are your assets aligned with you or against you?

Now what about the competition? Do you know their standards and practices? Do they pay slotting allowances to the national chains? Do they restock more frequently? Do they have better buyer incentives and allowances? Buyers are easily influenced by well-planned trade allowances. These are obstacles, threats to your objective.

What about the specialized needs of your customers? Are you communicating with the product development people back in the home office? Sam's Club, Costco, and other price clubs have unique requirements. Almost everybody knows by now that it does no good to treat them the same way you'd treat a supermarket, but you'd be surprised how many people try and fail. I know a company that has one of the fastest-selling home videotapes in the nation. Everywhere it's placed—catalogs, museums, discount retailers, or home video stores—it sells out in weeks. But did Sam's Club buy it? No. Sam's Club wanted a *twin* pack. And without that, there was no deal.

Identifying your threat is a complicated process, but in the end tracking down the obvious and the not-so-obvious market factors and internal practices that can shoot you down is key to achieving your mission objective.

STEP THREE: IDENTIFY YOUR SUPPORT ASSETS

Once you have your mission statement and know the competitive threats, scour your internal assets for the one thing that might make or break the sale.

Don't have any idea about advertising allowances or trade promotions? Unsure of your credit terms or return policies? Well, who's on your team? Have you ever taken inventory of the people around you who can help? You'd be surprised who's there. When I look around for help, I've got the entire Air Force behind me, but it took me a while to learn who was where. Let's take that hypothetical mission and the IADs map. If I'm the F–117 that is supposed to take out the C3i building, it would be nice to have help. So I'll call on support assets. First, I'll need to have a tanker airborne to get gas coming and going, and it wouldn't hurt to have a few of those F–15s in the air in case someone spots me and jumps my tail. Assuming I need them, I can roll them all straight into my mission plan.

But there are a dozen other support assets I can use—basic assets like the weaponeers who put the two bombs in the bomb bay, refuelers, maintainers, and electronics technicians. Do you know what is one of the most important support assets an F–117 pilot has? Even if you understand the technology that makes a Stealth plane work, it might surprise you to know that having a crew of skin maintainers makes all the difference. Any imperfections in a Stealth plane's surface—its skin—can compromise its stealth characteristics, so having a nice, smooth exterior is as important as the highest-tech instrument in the cockpit. As always, a successful mission is never a solo act.

The same is true in business. In any given company, there will be salespeople who think they're the F–15s, closing the deals and bringing the bottom line to the company. They think they have all the firepower they need right in their briefcases; the last thing they have time for is getting to know Betty in accounting back at the home office. But what a huge mistake—Betty may be just the person they need to help them land an account. If fighter pilots had that we-don't-need-help attitude, they would die. Even the hottest sticks in the sky would never survive, because they just can't do it alone. The network of threats is too diverse for one person to handle.

Ten years ago many of the mass retailers went to electronic ordering systems. They insisted that their vendors become capable of taking orders electronically. If you couldn't take orders electronically, you ran the risk of being thrown out of the store. No matter how good you were as a salesperson, how good your product, you were dead in the water without electronic ordering capabilities. And suddenly—for the first time in years—a lot of people needed to know more about their own internal support assets. *Who's in the information technology department? How quickly can we get up to speed?* Get to know your company from bottom to top, and you won't end up scrambling to catch up with the next opportunity—or missing it altogether.

The third part in your combat mission plan is to identify your support assets. Knowing your support assets before you need them can eliminate problems on the road to your mission objective. Don't be so arrogant as to think that your part of the business is the only part that makes the business go: Fighter pilots don't think that way. Bomber pilots don't think that way. And you can't afford to think that way. If you don't understand an area of your company, why not spend some time there? It's an investment in yourself, in the future of your company. Put the names of your primary support people on a crib sheet and look them over once a week and ask yourself: How can someone on this list help me tomorrow?

STEP FOUR: EMPHASIZE YOUR STRENGTHS AND THEIR WEAKNESSES

Never engage in a costly frontal attack when you can outflank the competition and still win.

We know our mission objectives, we've identified the threats, we've brought in the appropriate support assets; now we attack. What's the best way to go about it? The answer is simple: Apply your strengths against your competitor's weak points. The U.S. Air Force has inarguable strengths—outstanding training and superior, cutting-edge equipment. If we did nothing more imaginative than go head-to-head with our enemy in a mass merge of airplanes, we would undoubtedly win. But why do that? Why not be more creative, and design a plan that disables the enemy without exposing ourselves to so much danger?

We know, for example, that most of the world's air forces lag well behind us in night-fighting capability. They don't have infrared technology. They have few, if any, night vision goggles. Their pilots haven't been trained in night-fighting operations. Most of their ground defenses have diminished capability at night. These are profound and exploitable weaknesses.

Have you ever heard it said that the United States military "owns the night"? It's true. The United States is very proficient at night fighting. Our chopper pilots can fly at night, our F–15 and F–16 pilots can dogfight at night using night vision goggles, and our Stealth fighters and F–15E Strike Eagles have FLIR and DLIR (forward looking and downward looking infrared) displays. We're very comfortable at night, and our enemies aren't. So when do you think we would rather engage?

Night air combat is the perfect application of a strength against a weakness, and we used it effectively in the air campaign over Baghdad. In fact, the air war started at night. The first sign anyone had that our F–117s had attacked was the sound of bombs exploding. By the time the triple-A responded, the initial strike aircraft were long gone.

Polaroid is a classic example of a company that found a way to play its own strength against a competitive weakness. Rather than going head-to-head against Kodak in the 1950s, Dr. Edward Land isolated a weakness in its system. Regular film processing was time-consuming; after you took a picture, it seemed like forever before you could get it back from the developer and enjoy it.

Land's strength—instant film development in the camera—was applied to this weakness, and the Land Camera, with its Polaroid film, was an overwhelming success. Land launched an entire company by making a market in the folds of a competitive weakness. Can you think of others? What about FedEx (overnight delivery in a three-day delivery world), Schick (the *disposable* razor), even CNN (twenty-four-hour news).

The Air Force doesn't seek frontal engagements. Smart companies don't, either. When you analyze the competition, look for the kinds of creases, niches, and exploitable weaknesses that might provide a fertile ground for your own success. This is the fourth part of the combat mission plan: leveraging strengths and weaknesses.

STEP FIVE: SET YOUR TIMING

Once the plan is in place, the only thing left is to find the optimal moment to strike: Identify your optimal mission timing.

Once we know what the enemy's weakness is, and what we're going to throw at it, the next question is: When do we launch? We're always tempted to say, "Right now!" But that's not always the best answer. Indeed, there's always an optimal time to strike, and it's vitally important to find it. And more often than not, *environment* plays a deciding role.

Let's revisit our mission one more time. We're taking an F–117 downtown and attacking the C3i building with laser-guided munitions. All our support assets are scheduled to flow in after the Stealths, in a coordinated, precision-timed, air-to-air and air-to-ground campaign. We've got eight dark hours (10 P.M. to 6 A.M.) to pull this off. Just before "step time" (a term we use when we're ready to move to our aircraft) our weather man has come in and told us that clouds are reported over the target area. The mission is scrubbed. The entire package will stay on the ramp. Why? As you may remember, the Stealth fighter can do some remarkable things, but it absolutely needs one external factor in its favor to deliver its smart bombs—clear weather. When a smart bomb is dropped, it aims itself toward the glow made by a laser beam projected on the target. But the system doesn't work unless the bomb's sensor can detect the beam, and cloud cover is strong enough to obscure such a beam, rendering the feature absolutely useless.

Most of us have read about the agonizing days preceding the landing of Allied troops on the beaches of Normandy in June 1944. D-Day: The massive, complex and secret preparations had been completed by June 4, but when that day blew up a squall, and June 5 was just as bad, General Eisenhower was obliged to hold back his troops until the weather could clear. Eisenhower was well aware that neither the men nor the equipment could be held back indefinitely without serious consequences. He feared above all that German intelligence would detect the buildup and its location, and make defensive preparations accordingly. His instincts were to move and move quickly, preserving the element of surprise. But the bad weather brooked no argument: He had to wait. On June 6 the weather abated just enough to tip the scales in favor of the invasion, and the rest is history. Eisenhower's fears were justified: The water conditions on the sixth were still severe enough to cause many drowning deaths and sinking ships. To have launched on either of the previous days would have turned a harrowing victory into a disaster.

Timing is just as critical in a business environment. There's no point in taking a new golf ball to test market in December. You can't sell calendars in June. Mail order dives during the summer. Fitness and self-help products soar in January (all of those New Year's resolutions). Buyers at department stores load up with men's accessories in June, for Father's Day. Never try to make a sale to a buyer that has a blockbuster hit on his hands. All of his money will be in his inventory of *Titanic* home videos. *Part five, then, is to pick your timing carefully.*

STEP SIX: PLAN FOR CONTINGENCIES

It's far easier to work out your options in the quiet of your office than in the hectic battlefield.

We have a saying in the fighter pilot world: "Flexibility is the key to air power." When you're dealing with high technology and rapidly changing three-dimensional environments, you have to be flexible, adaptable, and fast on your feet. No matter how thoroughly you nail down the details, nothing ever goes exactly as planned. Technology lets you down. Equipment breaks. People make mistakes. Weather changes. The competition pulls a number on you.

The best way to survive the inevitable array of snafus is to plan for them ahead of time. Expect the unexpected. Practice your responses. Train for the unprecedented failure. Plan for that day when the impossible happens to you. For fighter pilots, this is basic. When we're traveling at 1,400 miles an hour and the program breaks down, we like to have at least two options at the ready—options we've rehearsed and trained to execute on some unlucky day.

Much of my training in the F–15 and most of my flying time in the 767 simulator (we call the sim a *sweat box*) has to do with emergency procedures or tactical contingencies. These are things like engine failures, battle damage, fuel leaks, electrical shutdowns, hydraulic leaks, fires, and ejections. As soon as they close me into the box, they start throwing one problem after the other my way—and they do it over and over until I get it right.

Similarly, during a mission briefing, which may last two hours, we spend about one third of our time talking about the what-ifs: What if the weather changes over the target? What if the air refueling tankers don't show up on time? What if the flight lead blows up on the way to the target? What if the threat shows up twice as strong as intel has told us? It is a lot easier for us to work out those decisions in the briefing room, sipping on a soft drink in an air-conditioned room, than it is two hours from now doing Mach 2, pulling nine G's, and trying to survive an SA–6 shot.

Business Contingency Planning

You can never eliminate surprise. There will always be times when you'll have to think fast and take appropriate action. But the ability to react *intelligently* to the unexpected *can* be taught and trained. There are no shortcuts here. To do this you have to break down the mission plan, spinning out all the possible scenarios and mapping out your responses. Sales forces do this better than almost any other corporate division. They call it overcoming objections. Salespeople will pepper each other with all the objections they can anticipate a buyer raising, going back and forth between themselves until they've pretty much thought through the best responses. When the meeting takes place, no one is ambushed by an unexpected question, no one is embarrassed by an unexpected objection. They're ready to close.

Contingency planning is a business priority, not a luxury. Even a cursory pass through a contingencies phase can eliminate embarrassing foul-ups. How many presentations have you attended only to find that the bulb didn't work on the data projector, or the computer crashed, or there weren't enough agendas for everybody because a few extra people showed up? It happens every day. A basic what-if list surely would have included, "What if the bulb burns out on the data projector?" Solution: Have an extra bulb handy. The trick is to have thought about it beforehand, rather than standing there flat-footed before a roomful of people who are thinking, "This poor guy."

When I traveled with my sales reps at Conco, I really put them to the test, especially when we were going into a closing meeting. What are the final objections likely to be? I would ask. How are you planning to overcome them? Where are the samples? Where are the extras? Where is the leave-behind if the buyer has to cancel the appointment?

Contingency planning is a big part of the airline industry. Just consider the problem of coordinating the interconnection of hundreds of flights a day, with several thousand crew members, all in motion, all subject to weather delays, equipment squawks (malfunctions), and airport holds. Airline scheduling is the ultimate game of probabilities and outcomes—and the last outcome the industry wants is a delayed or canceled flight. One way the industry handles it is to have crews on standby in case a scheduled crew is delayed. United Airlines keeps one group of reserve pilots on four-hour call, another group on two-hour call, and a third group of pilots on field standby reserve; they're ready for almost anything.

SUMMARY

Following the six steps for basic combat mission planning will give you a time-tested process for planning ahead—whether you're setting your company's five-year goals or planning your own for the day. Mission planning can make all the difference where it counts—in successful execution. Next time you're planning, review these six steps:

1. Define your mission objective, making it clear, measurable, attainable, and compliant with the overall objective.

2. Identify your primary threat and find out all you can about him, his equipment, and his doctrines. Then keep looking for the not-so-obvious threats. They're hiding out there, so put a lot of effort into finding them.

3. Find out who your support teams are and what they can do for you.

4. Lead with your strengths and pit them against the opponent's weak spots.

5. Don't launch until the timing is exactly right.

6. Talk, talk, talk about the what-ifs with everyone involved *before* the mission gets under way.

BRIEFING:
TAKING THE PLAN TO THE PEOPLE

DOBBINS AFB, SUMMER 1991. A DAY IN THE LIFE . . .

Four Killer Georgia Eagles (F–15s) sit on the ramp at Dobbins Air Force Base in Marietta, Georgia. They are parked side by side in a perfect line abreast formation. They are spaced exactly fifteen feet apart, one wingtip to the other. All four canopies are up; all four jets are ready to go.

Today these are my F–15s; this is my four-ship. I'm about to lead three men into battle, and I'm ready for it. The brief went well. The mission is clear. It's time to fly. I've given my pilots ten minutes to use the bathroom, make last-minute adjustments to their G-suits, and strap into their jets. From what you've read, you know by now that I don't expect them in their jets in eleven minutes. I expect them to be ready to go in *exactly* ten.

Sure enough, exactly ten minutes later we're all in. I look down the line at three pilots, strapped in and leaning into their oxygen masks. I twirl my index finger in a circle. Whoosh! All four F–15s start their APUs (auxiliary power units) at exactly the same moment. For the next few minutes we crank engines; run our ground checks, avionics checks, flight control checks, and weapons checks. The radar is sweeping, the INS (inertial navigation system) is cooking, and all of the lat-longs (navigational coordinates) are loaded for the air refueling track, the MOA (military operating area), the FEBA (forward edge of the battle area) and the bull's-eye. We check our AIM–9 missiles to make sure the seeker heads are cooled and ready to go. We make sure our AIM–7 Sparrows and our AMRAAMs are talking to our weapons control panel (PAX panel). We make a quick scan of all 350 switches and dials, and then I'm on the radio precisely ten minutes after engine startup.

"Cheetah One One check."

In ascending order and with crisp cadence, I expect to hear my four-ship check:

"Two."

"Three."

"Four."

But today I hear a pause, then "Three," then "Four." Hmm . . . no "Two." If someone doesn't check in, obviously he has a problem. Nobody's ever late for the check-in, not unless it's something serious. Does Two have a mission-critical problem? I get on the auxiliary radio.

"Two, say status."

Two answers that he'll be up in two minutes because he's working on an avionics problem. I look at my watch and make mental calculations. The delay is going to put us two minutes behind our takeoff time, which will put us two minutes behind our air refueling time, which means we won't be able to take on as much gas at the air refueling track as I hoped. We have to be in the MOA at our rendezvous point at *precisely* the right time since we're escorting a package of eight F–16s from the McIntyre Air National Guard Base over in Columbia, South Carolina. I have to make a decision. Either I have to leave without Two and let him catch up en route, or wait the two minutes and have all of us try to make it up en route.

Before I can make the decision I hear, "Two is up." All right! I start the check-in sequence again. They all check in.

Now I contact ground control on the radio: "Dobbins ground, Cheetah One One ready to taxi four Killer Georgia Eagles with alpha." It may be corny to call us Killer Eagles, but I like to pump it up a bit. We Eagle drivers don't take prisoners, and it doesn't hurt to float a little pride over the radio. Ground responds to my

check-in, knows I have the correct weather and runway information because I used the word "alpha," and gives us permission to
taxi.

Again, precision counts. I expect my four-ship to move in an
exact, synchronized fashion. I release brakes and pull out, then
Two, Three, and Four fall in behind me with perfect spacing. We
look sharp, no ragged edges. That's exactly what I want. If our
taxiing is sloppy or our radio comm is sloppy, then our mission is
going to be sloppy. If Four gets behind, I am going to get on the
radio and say, "Four, push it up and get into position." I want to set
the discipline and the standards right away, right there on the
ground. Maybe Four hasn't flown in a while. Maybe he's a one-star
general. It doesn't matter to me. I am the flight lead, and I'm the
boss. I want everybody to know that this is not going to be a
sloppy flight.

Before we get onto the runway, we swing around in another line
abreast "hold" and I look down the formation. Yes, every one of
our helmets is lined up perfectly. Now it's time to arm the
weapons. I look down at the ramp. A whole team of people is out
there getting ready for us on the armament pad. We put our hands
in the air to let them know we're in no danger of hitting a pickle
button—that is, a launch button—or any other life-threatening
switch in the cockpit. When the armament guys see eight hands in
the air, they start pulling pins and yanking off missile caps and
doing their work to arm our weapons.

Then, when everybody is ready, Four turns and gives a thumbs-
up to Three, who passes it to Two, who passes it up to me. Click!
We all turn on our landing lights at exactly the same moment. I
call the tower and say, "Cheetah One One number one ready." The
tower responds, "Roger, Cheetah One One, taxi into position and
hold." With precision, four F–15s release brakes and taxi onto the
runway. Now, the runway at Dobbins is a little narrow, and the
wingspan of the F–15 is forty-two feet. Nonetheless, we have a
method of overlapping our wings so that we can get all four aircraft on the runway together, but positioned so that when we run
up the power, exhaust nozzles aren't going to be pointing at any-

one. I expect to see this special configuration when we get into position for the takeoff. Sure enough, we look sharp.

The tower then says, "Cheetah One One, cleared for takeoff, fly runway heading, climb to 3,000 feet, contact departure on button five." I'll say, "Tower, Cheetah One One cleared for takeoff," but I don't need to say anything to my four-ship because they're all looking at me. I just turn and twirl my right hand, which means run 'em up. All four Eagles start pushing their power up to 80 percent. Forty-two thousand pounds of thrust thunder out of our nozzles. As the jet shakes around me, the feeling in the cockpit becomes one of pure energy. We all know that if we gave it any more gas, we'd burn out our brakes. (In the F–15 the engines are so powerful that if you push them up to 100 percent—what we call *military power*—the brakes can't hold the aircraft on the runway.) So we push the power up to 80 percent and check to make sure both engines are running and that our instruments are in the green. If they are, Four will nod, Three will nod, and Two will nod. Everyone's engines are good to go. I tap my helmet, move my head to the back of my seat rest, then nod forward. That's the signal. Two, my wingman, and I will take off together.

As my helmet comes forward, I release my brakes and my wingman does, too. We're off! In a matter of seconds we're both going 120 knots down the runway, our wingtips just three feet apart. I gently pull back the stick and rotate ten degrees nose high. At the same instant, my wingman rotates his jet, too. How does he know to do this? Because he isn't looking at the runway—he isn't even looking straight ahead. My wingman is always looking at me. Wherever I go, he goes. He does what I do, always managing our separation. When he sees my flight controls deflect and my nose starting to rotate, he does the exact same thing. It's trust at the highest level. It's his life and my life on the line.

Once we're off the ground, I'll nod and we'll both pull our gear handles and suck up the landing gear at the exact same instant. This is done for more than show. The landing gear creates drag; when the gear comes up, the F–15 slips through the air a little quicker. We could easily pull apart, but by pulling our gear at the same time, my wingman never gets out of position; he's right there, three feet off my wing, his helmet facing my jet.

It's a good thing because on this flight we have a cloud deck at 500 feet, and we immediately enter the soup. Now we're in close formation and I'm navigating and maintaining aircraft control for us both. Moreover, two F–15s are coming up behind us. No problem. We planned on twenty-second spacing. Twenty-second spacing gives us exactly two miles between the lead element (me and my wingman) and the trail element.

Even so, as soon as the trail element takes off, the number three man (who is the deputy flight lead) and the number four man lock on to me with their radars. Since I'm in the clouds they can't see me, and the only way they can stay in formation is by radar lock. Three lets me know all is well, telling me, "Three is tied." When I hear that, I look at my radar to make sure I have a symbol, which we call a spike, in the shape of a small wing, which means that the airplane behind me is an F–15. Now I know the F–15 is locked on to me at my six o'clock position and that he's roughly two miles behind me. We'll be safe as we transition the clouds.

I expect to come out of this deck fairly quickly, and sure enough a few beats later I'm on top and into VMC (visual meteorological conditions). Just as quickly, I hear "Cheetah Three is visual," which tells me the trailing two-ship is out of the clouds, too. I say, "Roger, Three. Rejoin tactical left side." As soon as I say "tactical," my wingman will break out to 6,000 feet line abreast formation. Three will bring his two-ship up with mine, also at 6,000 feet abreast, and soon we'll have four aircraft spread four miles wide, line abreast, ready to go to war. You can hear the bugles calling for the cavalry. Plant the flag and fight!

I couldn't help but look up and down the line as we flew. It really was a fantastic sight. Here I was, a twenty-seven-year-old farm boy, pulling oxygen from my oxygen mask, one hand on the stick, one on the throttles, three jets pushing through the sky beside me, together packing more firepower than a whole squadron of WWII-era fighters. I swelled with pride. We were only five minutes into our mission and the execution had been near flawless. The Killer Georgia F–15s were up—and they were *mine*.

THE MISSION BRIEFING

Of course, none of this happened by accident. This intricate, precise ballet of jets was made entirely possible by an hour-and-a-half preflight meeting called a *mission briefing*. The mission briefing is one of the bedrock procedures in the Air Force. On it hinges every aspect of a successful mission, a safe mission, an effective mission. It is as fundamental to flying combat as the jet itself. It is one of the pillars on which the fighter pilot way rests. It is a deadly serious, near-sacred event during which the leader (the flight lead) lays out the complete details of a mission—the who, what, where, when, and why of everything that will happen from the moment we step out of the briefing room to the moment we pop our canopies and spool down the engines after it's over. Let me repeat: On this briefing hinges *everything*—from the procedures we'll use to taxi onto the runway to the ultimate success of the mission itself—and as the flight lead, it's my job to lay it all out, to tell the four-ship everything we need to know.

BRIEFINGS VERSUS MEETINGS

First, let me clarify some terminology. To call the briefing a *meeting* does it an injustice. Meetings happen every day. Meetings are a necessary part of any organization's communications network, and many times they are impromptu and circumstantial. But a briefing is something different. A briefing occurs by prearrangement immediately before the operations people begin to execute the combat mission plan, which we discussed in the preceding chapter. A briefing is the place where the mission objective makes its last stop, the time when the pilots receive their specific instructions. A briefing is tactical. A briefing is about execution. *A briefing is the buy-in point for the men and women who will put their lives on the line.*

Does it have a counterpart in business? Not entirely, and that's the point. Business has its *missions*—sales meetings, regional meetings, kickoffs, store openings, and such—but not always the *briefings* that should precede them. That's a mistake. We in the fighter pilot community have come to learn that the secret of a successful mission is always a thorough briefing, just as a poorly executed mission can almost always be traced back to a poor—or truncated—briefing. Because we simply can't survive too many bad missions, we've been taught a briefing process that follows certain principles which, when adhered to, will put a *motivated* wing of pilots into the air, help them *successfully* execute their mission, and bring them back alive. The truth is, businesses want the same outcomes for their missions—a motivated team bringing back successful results—but too many of them skip the brief. Briefing—and debriefing, which we will discuss in chapter 11—needs to be a part of your *everyday operating procedures*. As you'll see in the following pages, briefings can be one of the most powerful business tools you can borrow from the fighter pilot community. First, though, let's look at the hows and whys.

FORM AND STRUCTURE

There is absolutely nothing random about a briefing; there is no frantic free-flow of information in the manner of a boisterous "boiler room" company meeting, nor is there any free discussion of objectives or strategies. There is a time-tested structure to a proper mission briefing, and it must be adhered to rigidly. Make no question about it—a briefing is planned, methodical, quiet, and intense. The door opens exactly when the briefing is supposed to start and everybody is on time. The room is neat and orderly—no clutter. The flight lead stands, the wingmen sit. Presentation boards are arrayed in logical positions throughout the room; the writing is neat and easy to read; flight paths are drawn out and the lines of text are ruler-straight. If the briefer intends to use AV equipment, it's in place, prefocused on the screen, and has been checked and rechecked (with a spare light bulb). No questions are asked until the lead solicits them, or until the end of the briefing.

When I walk into a combat mission briefing, I can see whether the flight lead has been there one hour, two hours, or three, and whether he's spent six to eight hours before that thinking about our mission. This initial impression of the room is vitally important. It's nearly impossible to shake a bad first impression; a good first impression, on the other hand, always gets me on board fast. If the flight lead has done his work, it'll show! Would I be willing to follow that guy into combat? Absolutely.

On the other hand, I've been to lousy mission briefings: briefings that started late, briefings where the flight lead was still writing bullet points on the board when we arrived and had no backup plan when the AV crashed. What do you think the buy-in was like for those missions? That briefer may have been the greatest fighter pilot in the squadron, but he was rushed, the briefing went off late, his flight members came in late, and even as they left to head to their jets and begin the mission they found there were questions left unanswered.

Briefings set the standard and the tone for the mission. If the meeting is sloppy and the briefing is sloppy, you can be assured that the execution will be sloppy, too.

The same thing is true of business briefings. Time and again people have come up to me after a seminar and told me their own disaster stories of meetings gone bad: A key presentation was poorly prepped, making the team look foolish; a key account review got started late, with bungled graphics; an annual sales meeting degenerated into a sloppy, jerky, start-and-stop affair. That's just the kind of thing that can be avoided by a thorough premeeting briefing.

Think back to your last business meeting. Maybe the occasion was the opening of a new bank branch, a new restaurant, or a new store. Did you have a briefing before the event? Was it formal? If it was, were you given a briefing time stated in advance? Did the meeting actually start on time? Did your leader prep the boards in four different colors so they were segmented by topic, easy to read and understand? Did he go over his computer presentation and make sure his software was feeding images to the projector properly? Was it apparent that the presenter came in two or three hours earlier to prepare, giving everyone a sense of his purpose and determination? As soon as you walked into the room, were you impressed enough to follow that guy all the way to downtown Baghdad, based on what you'd seen in the first five seconds? Did he lead by example and set the tone?

A briefing is led by one person, the flight lead, who's clearly spent hours laying out the details of the mission, preparing his visual materials for the presentation, prepping his assistants, and readying the room. In a sense the briefing represents the calm before the storm, and when it's properly conducted, everyone inevitably realizes that the seeds of the mission's success were sown in the briefing.

1. First Impressions—Setting the Standard

The mission briefing is all about empowering people, about triggering an enthusiastic response, about giving people the tools they need to execute their tasks immediately—and *successfully*. And to achieve these ends it's crucial to set high standards for every element of the briefing itself, no matter how minor. Start with attendance. First, specify a time and a place for the briefing—let's say 0830 (8:30 A.M.). Then make it clear that you expect 100 percent attendance, promptly at 0830. Let people know you don't mean they should be milling about in the room sometime around then; you want people seated and looking eyes front at 8:30 sharp.

Then, by all means, make sure the meeting starts on time. Shut the door, walk to the front, and start talking. Sure, for the first few briefings you hold this way people will be late, but if you keep the standards high, that won't last too long. No one likes to be the last person to sneak into a meeting that's already under way—and good people won't do it twice.

Next, let it be known exactly how long the briefing will last. If the briefing starts at 0830 and it's supposed to end at 1000 hours, end it at 1000 hours. Period. If this is your first brief, practice it at home or in your hotel room until it works within the allotted time. *Never, ever brief longer than scheduled.* (How many times have you been to meetings that have gone on for hours and hours? Nothing is a bigger turnoff than a tediously long meeting—and no one is less popular than the leader who drags it on.) Start on time, end on time—do what you said you were going to do—and people will know they can rely on you.

Have the Visuals Prepared   People follow along better and comprehend more if you use visuals. Use as many visuals as possible. I use computers, whiteboards, photographs, and maps. I direct people's eyes to and from the important material. I weave it together, but always come back to a visual, always providing my audience with a focal point for each important concept or idea. It's a long-established fact: People can assimilate and retain more information when words and pictures are combined.

Prep the room with the equipment and props you'll need to present efficiently and effectively—but keep it interesting. If you're using whiteboards, try using different color markers for different subjects. Make sure you write neatly, and don't forget to write *large enough* that the general with glasses in the back of the room can read every word. Always read your words exactly as you wrote them on the board, *then* ad-lib: Nothing confuses people more than not knowing where you are on the board. Use a ruler to make the lines straight and make your board look neat and orderly.

An important note here. If you are the leader, do the visuals yourself. Don't delegate this work to someone else. This is your opportunity to visualize the mission—to truly see it in your mind and to work out problems that might crop up while executing. This is classic visualization—an invaluable process that all good flight leaders use.

Make sure you don't put your entire briefing on the board. You do want an outline up there, for your benefit as well as theirs, but don't try to say it all. Use bullet points to direct the flow of your presentation. Acronyms and abbreviations are okay, even encouraged, but don't become a reader. Leap from your bullet points to your audience and rake them with eye contact.

Caveat   Before you delve into the oral briefing itself, you have to set an important ground rule. Because your information is so tightly interrelated, you must make it clear that questions should be held until the very end at the meeting, or until those moments when you specifically ask for them. Ask the participants not to hold their hands up or interrupt. A good briefing weaves information together. Questions asked at the wrong time can interrupt a critical, interlocking sequence of events. Tell them to write their questions down and wait. Make sure this is understood.

The Line-up Card   There are a few tricks we use to help us keep our information ordered for a briefing, and one of them is the line-up card. Before a briefing starts, I hand out five-by-seven cards to each crew member, each preprinted with categories of information for them to fill in as the briefing progresses. When are we going to step to the jets? When are we going to take off? What are the tactical scenarios we might encounter? There's a place for each piece of information, and this gives the pilots a way to organize their notes—and helps me make sure that the details of my brief will be clear and easily recalled in the heat of battle. The line-up card is a terrific tool, and it works as well in the waiting room before a major presentation as it does in the cockpit.

Briefing in Groups   I have been asked by many of our clients whether briefings can be conducted by a team of people, rather than just one person. Absolutely—it's something we often do in the fighter pilot community. Every briefing can be broken down into its logical parts, and the responsibility for briefing those parts can be divided among the team members. Each member then can have a distinct role in the briefing. Splitting the brief into parts has a nice benefit—it ensures that several members of the crew are especially comfortable with the mission before it begins. But even if three or four of you conduct the briefing, there's one important thing to remember—there is only *one* flight lead. He's still in charge of the brief, directs the tactics, and remains responsible for the mission outcome.

2. Establishing the Mission Objective

The most important thing you will say in your mission briefing is what you say in the very first sentence. Consider the moment. People have arrived on time, they see a room that is perfectly prepped with all sorts of visuals and information, but they have absolutely no frame of reference to help them understand where all this is going. You want to fill them in as soon as possible, to get everyone on the same page as soon as possible.

Primary Objective Accordingly, the first thing you should announce is your objective. "Today our mission objective is to provide air superiority (a specific action) over the Snowbird MOA (a specific place) starting at 0400 ZULU to 0600 Z (a specific time)."

Now stop right there and ask if there are any questions. Is that objective clear? Remember, the mission objective needs to be understandable, measurable, attainable, and support the overall goal of the organization. Are there any questions? Did everyone understand every word you said? You want any gray areas cleared up right away.

The Scenario Next, brief (that is, give a briefing on) the scenario, the situational analysis, and the background. This helps the team members place the mission in context. For training missions, we present trainees with a variety of scenarios, usually based on a plausible reality. Here's an example I've used:

After the Gulf War, Saddam Hussein is not deposed. In fact, he realigns with other rogue nations to plan an air strike into Israel. It's a quick way to involve the United States in another expensive foreign deployment and to disrupt world peace. The President and his Joint Chiefs have decided that we need an immediate presence in the area. The President orders aircraft carriers into the region and has assigned our fighter squadron to deploy and provide air superiority over this area (simulated by the Snowbird MOA), thus preventing them from launching their strike fighters without engaging us first.

This scenario is a terrific motivator; there isn't a pilot in the Air Force who couldn't see how it fits in with the overall objectives of the United States.

Secondary Objectives   If you have them (and businesses almost always do), you'll want to cover any secondary objectives next. For example, our mission objective is to provide air superiority, but we may have some other objectives to accomplish along the way—goals like ensuring 100 percent success of all our shots; ensuring that each bandit is sorted before our shots are fired; ensuring that each person has identified friend or foe before he releases a missile. These, too, should be clear, measurable, and attainable, and support the overall vision of the organization—but also fit within the parameters of the mission-specific objective.

3. The Time Hack

Time is a factor in every mission we undertake, and the same must hold for you. It doesn't matter if you're a fighter pilot or a traveling salesman: Timing is something we all live with. Coordinating clocks is the next part of the brief. We all pull out our watches and make sure that everyone is coordinated to the same second. In the movies they'd call that *synchronizing your watches*; we call it a *time hack*. We all have to be hacked off of the same clock. We'll be taking off, hitting the tanker, and arriving on-station based on precise timing.

Timing is well understood in the business world but not always in ways we notice. TV commercials are cut in thirty-second increments. Radio commercials are cut in sixty-second intervals. Airliners take off on the minute. And no one likes a tardy meeting.

But in a bigger sense, timing can fall way out of whack and kill vital corporate initiatives. In traveling the nation speaking to businesses, I've heard countless stories of gross timing failures—and among the most frequent are variations of that awful story in which two departments get out of sync with each other in the midst of a new product introduction. The scenario invariably seems to go like this: R&D has created a new product and tested it to make sure it works, and the good buzz begins inside the company. The salespeople hear about it, and they're excited. They can't help themselves; they leak the wonderful news to their accounts. They're jazzed, too. All of a sudden, here come the orders. But the company isn't ready for orders! It hasn't even started mass production, and certainly hasn't laid the distribution pipeline. The company tells its key accounts that it will be another month or two before the product reaches the market, and *poof!* The sound the company hears is the air going out of its balloon.

The record and movie industries are more alert to this problem than perhaps any other sector in the nation, with software companies closing in fast. To manage timing issues, they have something called *street dates*. Everything is worked back from the street date—the advertising schedule, the day the trucks leave the warehouses for the retailers, the lead time to manufacture inventories, the lead time to produce freestanding displays; all of it works back from that one single time hack. Thus, when there's a new film or a new rock CD (or a hot new book or a new software upgrade) about to hit the market, the advertising campaigns will have been written, produced, and placed to run, the newspaper and magazine reviewers will have gotten their copies and have slotted their reviews for the week *before* the ad campaign—and on the announced street date, the doors will open to lines of people waiting to buy a copy.

Can you see how important it is that everybody understands the timeline of a given mission? Then make sure everyone on your team's working off the same time hack—whether it means everybody showing up for a group presentation on time, or everybody working toward the same street date.

4. Weather and Environment

After the time hack, we tell our flight members what kind of weather they're going to be flying in and what the "environment" will be—in terms of geography, attitude, and other factors. For weather briefings, I'll either invite a weather person in to give us the expert view, or I'll go to the weather shop and prepare myself to do the brief alone. Whoever does it, we'll touch on *all* the weather that could affect our mission—on departure, on the route to the MOA, in the engagement area itself, on the air refueling track, and on our return to base. Weather can affect any phase of flight, so we don't skip the easy parts—the coming and going to the target area.

There's a parallel here on a surprisingly literal level: In the retail environment, weather can be a hugely important factor, particularly if the mission involves outside activities, such as the fanfare surrounding a new store opening, or if it requires a minimum number of attendees, such as at a special purchase sale or a heavy promotion. Event promoters probably sweat the weather more than any other people in the world, but most have contingency plans for rainy or snowy days. (I once saw an air show organizer order his pyrotechnics crews to set off all their fireworks from the ground after the planes were grounded, just to give the few spectators a show.) How will you adjust to weather problems? You can't if you don't do a weather check.

Next, I'll brief the environment. This is broken down into two parts—the physical environment and the attitudinal environment. For us, the physical, geographical environment is critical, so I'll cover it carefully. If there are mountains in the area I'll discuss the topographic features, or, better still, I'll show pictures and use maps. People need reference points before embarking, and it's important that my crew be familiar with their mission environment, particularly if the geography is threatening or can be used to the enemy's advantage.

For business applications, too, geography can be make-or-break. McDonald's and Marriott are both brilliant at site selection. Their experts have learned to eyeball roads, housing tracts, the proximity of schools, even the length and duration of traffic signals, and from those physical attributes calculate a new store's potential on a prospective site. The entire wireless industry lives and dies on its cell zone coverage, and the process of identifying the best sites for cell towers is crucial to good customer service and a clean signal. Physical attributes can be important on a smaller level, too: New technology now allows retail stores to change product prices by radio signal without a store clerk actually touching the shelves, but for these amazing new devices to work, the transmitters hidden in the ceilings must have an unobstructed line-of-sight to the individual gondolas—a contingency store managers have to keep in mind at all times.

After the physical brief, I'll brief my pilots on attitudinal factors and other X factors—how our enemy *feels* about us, how they *feel* about the United States, their degree of *animosity* toward us, and their degree of commitment to the fight.

This is the kind of "state of mind" environment check every business should have. For global corporations, an awareness of cultural attitudes is crucial; any company planning to sell into new markets has to study each new culture closely enough to be able to anticipate how a product will be perceived by its people. And the subtleties can go far beyond matters of price or competition. For example, in Spain there's a particular cigarette brand that has traditionally been favored over all the others simply because for years the King of Spain smoked them, so American brands have been hard put to make a dent in that market. In Taiwan, on the other hand, an American brand is a status symbol and a cigarette's advertising must have American imagery, not Chinese, or the product has no chance.

Closer to home, an environmental briefing on domestic sales is the kind of forum where regional U.S. buying habits and histories would naturally come up. Home Depot, for example, has broken down the nation into nine U.S. buying regions, each reflecting the distinct buying habits of different areas of the country. Regional buyers, being closer to the retail environments they serve, can track those buying idiosyncrasies and stock the right products for each store better than a centralized buyer can in a distant home office. These are the kinds of attitudinal factors that every company must learn, to keep some overlooked factor from dooming a mission before it has a chance to succeed.

Finally, a business environment briefing should address the general economic outlook in the area under discussion. No marketing plan, production plan, or sales forecast can exist independent of an assessment of the general economic health of a market, retailer, region, or country. This part of a good business brief should include a picture of the overall factors—internal and external—that can have as much effect on a product's sales as any of its inherent attributes.

5. Motherhood (Squadron Standards/Administration)

Of all the segments of an Air Force briefing, by far the oddest-sounding one is the part we call *motherhood*. That's the word we use to describe our squadron standards—the things we have to keep in mind on *every* mission, the equivalent of a business's standard operating procedures. These are our principles, our everyday procedures, our expected mode of flying for everyday phases of flight: how many seconds apart we are on takeoff, the order in which we refuel, the rundown of emergency procedures. These all come under the heading of motherhood—the kinds of things your mother always thought you wouldn't remember once she'd sent you off to school (*Did you remember to bring your lunch? Do your homework? Say "thank you" and "please"?*). To confirm that standard operating procedures are in place for a given aspect of a mission, the flight lead will tell us that "motherhood is in effect" for that aspect of the plan. And if there's some reason to break from established practice, the briefing is when the flight members would hear about it.

The equivalent of motherhood in corporate life is your basic professional code of standards. TDI, a national outdoor advertising company, has a set of motherhood standards that specify not only what kind of jacket its reps wear on sales calls, but the very tie pin they wear in their lapels. Ritz-Carlton hotel employees are famous for their service—and well they should be, for their service standards are codified down to the last detail. Next time you're in a Ritz-Carlton hotel, try it out by presenting a problem to a passing employee: No matter whom you turn to, that person will stop, look you in the eye, try to understand your question, and then try even harder to find an answer. (How far can they take it? Put it this way: The doorman probably knows the menus for each of the hotel's restaurants.)

6. The Threat

After covering motherhood, we turn to the threat—the military equivalent of your business competition. To do that, I may invite the intelligence officer to come in to help with the briefing. If it's a training mission, I will create a threat scenario beforehand in accordance with the training objective of our mission. Often I telephone the "adversary" squadron—we often use the Marine F/A–18s out of Beaufort, South Carolina, as sparring partners—and talk to their flight lead. I'll ask him to give us MiG–29 simulations during our engagement. Then I'll create several imaginary surface-to-air missile sites and put them on the map.

When I brief the threat, I'll tell the pilots about the SAM sites on the ground, and we have to stay clear of their effective radiuses. If anyone wanders over those sites, he's automatically dead and has to go home.

Even though we all know what it looks like, I may put a picture on the wall and explain our adversary's equipment: *This is a MiG–29, this is how high it can fly, this is how fast it can fly; we know it's carrying these weapons, this is how far it can shoot.*

Then I turn to our defenses: *This is what we're going to see on our radar warning receiver when we've been locked by a MiG; this is what we'll see when an AA–10 Alamo short burn missile has been fired at us,* and so on. This is repetitive material, for the most part, but it helps keep us current.

I'll also brief as much as I know about the people driving the MiGs—the pilots. This is where the human factor comes in. What are the pilots going to be like when we meet them at the merge? How are they trained, what do they know about our jets, what's their motivation—how desperate are they to win? What's their psychological makeup—pussycat or psycho? As much as possible I want to know the heart, the soul, and the gut of the men or women driving the adversary jets: This kind of knowledge can be more important than the capability of their jets.

Threats should be a major part of any business brief. In fact, this is one area where businesses are likely to be dealing with more adverse possibilities than we do during an air-to-air mission. How often do you review the dozens of objections that a buyer might pose? How often do you go through the problems a customer may have with your service? How desperate is your competitor? How much lead time does your technology really have (probably not much, in this digital age)? Will your competitors do *anything* to stay alive? Will they lie to your customers? Will they sabotage your sales events? Are they likely to start rumors in the press, or pull other dirty tricks? Going over every contingency and possible threat will help keep you ahead of the game, just as surely as it helps keep us in the air.

7. Tactics

Next—and most important by far—comes our discussion of tactics. In an Air Force briefing, we spend 75 percent of our time on tactics. This is what the pilots need to hear; this is what they're there for. We don't waste half our time on standards (that's what the shorthand concept of motherhood is for), weather/environment, or even the threat—and neither should you. What you should really concentrate on is tactics—how to win the ball game.

The tactical brief is the leader's time to shine. This is where he will be closely watched and measured by his team. This is where he combines individuality with practice, science with art. Why? Because he'll be using the team's specialized tools—missiles, radar, altitude, speed, routes of ingress and egress—to execute a specific mission. For a sales manager the tools might be sales qualifiers, product knowledge, closing tactics, a new catalog, or a new product attribute; whatever they may be, everyone in the room will know all about them and have an opinion on how to do things best—but the leader's plan is the only one that counts.

In this section, the focus is on the specifics of the potential engagement. Not takeoffs and landings. Not refueling. Nothing to do with motherhood. This is the backbone of the mission, the real reason we're getting into the jets. Here's where we talk about guns and missiles. Here's where I tell the pilots the exact formation we're going to fly, when we're going to lock our missiles, how we're going to fire them, how we're going to determine whether we're offensive or defensive, when we're going to engage, reengage, or disengage. We go through every scenario the enemy might throw at us, and we go over just exactly how we intend to win in each one.

So complex and important is this part of the briefing that we have a special subsection for it. It's called a *decision matrix*. The decision matrix is a grid that gives us guidelines for the tough decisions we'll need to make quickly as we get into the heat of battle. As fighter pilots, we have to understand the variables that dictate whether we're offensive, defensive, or neutral against an enemy, whether we should engage, and, if we engage, whether we should launch a missile or go to guns. In the ever-changing environment of air combat, the decision matrix helps us make these life-and-death choices *without having to stop and think.*

The decision matrix breaks up the line-of-flight of each mission into discrete intervals—forty, thirty, twenty, fifteen, twelve, ten, and five miles, for example, from the point where we meet with our adversary. On that line-of-flight, our jets will be flying Mach 1, which is roughly ten miles a minute; the MiGs will be flying at the same speed, which means the distance between us is closing at a rate of twenty miles a minute. At those speeds, we don't have time to think through a lot of options. That's why I want my pilots to know exactly what to expect and exactly what to do at each of the mileage markers leading up to the threat. At forty miles, for instance, I'll double-check that our formation is in good tactical formation; at thirty miles, when we encounter blips on the radar, my men will have to identify them as friend or foe; at twenty-five miles we'll lock onto the targets; at twenty miles, after sorting our targets to make sure no two men have locked on the same target, we'll fire our missiles.

At fifteen miles to the threat we enter what we call the *decision range*. This is the most important moment in air combat: Our missiles are traveling toward the enemy, but their missiles are probably coming toward us, too. Each of us has only a few seconds to decide whether we're winning, losing, or neutral—whether his missile will hit the enemy before the enemy's missiles hits him. This will vary by pilot in the formation, so each pilot runs through the predefined decision matrix at fifteen miles, doing a lightning-fast evaluation of his current situation and judging his best next step according to the rules set forth in the matrix. If I'd stipulated that this was a low-risk mission—meaning under no circumstances did we want to lose an F–15—then the pilots would know that if even one pilot found himself in a defensive position we'd automatically abort. If we were in a high-risk mission, on the other hand, the defensive F–15 would use a specialized set of tactics to break his adversary's radar lock, then reengage.

At ten miles we start the "tally-ho"—which means the pilots start trying to find the targets with their eyeballs—and pull their throttles back to cool their engines down, to help thwart the adversary's heat-seeking missiles. And ten miles isn't very far when you're flying as fast as we are; before we know it we're in the merge—coming beak to beak with the adversary—and ready to decide whether to plant the flag and turn and burn with the bandits (dogfight), or blow straight through. Every one of these decisions is made according to the set of conditions stipulated in the matrix. Even after the merge we're still using the matrix as our guide, doing ninety-degree check turns to make sure no one sneaks up on us, then converging at a rendezvous point (or get-well point) before we head home.

That may seem like a lot to digest. But is your mission any less important than mine? Haven't we established that it's either your fork in the steak or the other guy's? Businesses need to think through their important events with the same precision and attention to detail that we fighter pilots bring to our missions. Focus on the critical waypoints for your business mission and create your own decision matrix that takes into account your or your team's progress through the mission. Things always have a timeline. Maybe your critical waypoints are time hacks—the time of a store opening, the crunch time at lunch hour, or the influx of hotel guests at 6 P.M. Fashion your tactics, identify the critical waypoints, then build a decision matrix that allows people to respond instantaneously, in the midst of the mission, to almost any contingency.

8. Brief the Contingencies

Just as in the previous chapter, you must brief the what-ifs—contingencies not only in the tactical phases of the flight, but in the administrative phases as well. Again, this is one of the most critical things you can do.

9. Conclusion of the Brief

In the last part of the briefing, you summarize the key points of the mission, then ask for questions. Is anybody unclear about the mission objective? Is anybody uncertain about the weather, the threat, our motherhood? Does anybody have questions on contingencies? If there are none . . . okay, let's go! It can be a good sign if there are no questions—that indicates that the brief was comprehensive. But now you really should *encourage* questions: They set the stage for the debrief, which we'll discuss later. Make certain no one leaves the room until you—and they—are sure of what everyone is supposed to do.

USING THE BRIEF IN YOUR BUSINESS

A mission brief can be held for a big group, but most often it is not. The most effective briefs involve four to eight people, and are limited to those who will actually be executing a particular mission together. In other words, this is not a company-wide meeting. This is an execution-level event.

Although the briefing is most commonly used by operations teams such as sales and customer service, other units of your combat-ready organization—sales support, logistics, communications—can also have briefings on the particular missions they must undertake. The briefing, after all, is the place where everyone's job is defined and made concrete.

The protocols of the mission briefing can provide an administrative structure that enables a lot of information to be passed along in a minimum amount of time, with a maximum degree of understanding, no matter what your job is in the organization.

But the briefing's value extends far beyond its administrative efficacy. The whole structure of the briefing is designed to set the tone for perfect execution. How? One word: attitude. When the employees see how diligent and prepared the briefer is, they get the sense that *they're* important—and that what they're doing is important, too. They quickly realize that the briefer has gone the extra mile not for his own glorification but to help them do their jobs better. By the time the brief is over, the attendees should feel committed, enthusiastic, totally bought-in, and *vitally important* to the successful outcome of the mission.

The briefing is a dynamic event. I've given you the basic structure and progression of a good briefing in the paragraphs above, but there is nothing like experience to help you get them right. In our Afterburner Seminars we teach the basics of briefing, then ask people to conduct a military-style mission briefing based on scenarios we invent. When managers and executives conduct the brief, we find a consistent result: They express themselves beautifully, are poised and confident in front of the group, and have a good command of the mission objectives. But by and large their first attempts at briefings are failures. First, they tend to deliver the whole brief too quickly. Although given twenty minutes to cover everything, the executives' average briefing time is seven minutes! They have a lot of information to impart; they tend to try to blurt it all out too quickly. A slower speaking pace is a product of experience. In time, they learn to speak at a speed that allows employees to take in the information more easily.

Second, the executives' briefings tend to focus almost exclusively on the big picture. The objective is clear, the environment is accurate, the strategy and tactics are sound—but at the end of the briefing no one is sure what to do. This is a fundamental error. A briefing is nothing if not a set of definitive instructions on who does what, when, and how. Without that, the briefing has no value. We spend a lot of our Afterburner time getting business briefers to be much more specific with their instructions.

Third, briefers tend to skimp on their visual preparation. They are accustomed to verbalizing their instructions. When given the time and materials to add visual impact to their briefings, managers still underuse them. This, too, is something that can be corrected in time.

If you take the time to integrate a regular, well-oiled briefing system into your business—and train your managers to deliver their briefings thoroughly and effectively—you'll be giving your company an unbeatable secret weapon in the combat of business. The practice has already begun gaining ground in the business world; companies involved in process applications, for example, have often found a briefing system to be essential to their execution of their specific mission. But no one can match the briefing process used by Sapient Corporation. Sapient is a young public company that integrates mainframes and disparate software programs into complex, integrated, and *functioning* systems for blue-chip clients like Wells Fargo and the state of Maine. It's not an easy thing to do. In fact, its industry is plagued by cost and deadline overruns. Sapient, however, has distinguished itself by delivering 90+ percent of its projects on time and on budget. And one key to its success is a morning brief and an end-of-day debrief—*every day a project team is working on a job*. Not just a brief at the beginning and a debrief two months later. Every day begins with a brief of the day's objectives, and ends with a debrief analyzing how well they did. The next morning, it starts again with a brief to reiterate that day's mission objectives and ends with a debrief. The process allows Sapient to ensure that no one gets too far off track, or off budget. (Its briefing room standards exceed even those of the fighter pilot community, and those standards apply to employees *and* customer alike—if you're late, you toss $5 in the hat. No cell phones, no interruptions.)

I made lots of mistakes when I became a flight lead and had to start briefing missions. I forgot basic flight protocols on some occasions, did a lot of on-the-job learning on others. It took me a while before I had it in me to deliver my plans with calm confidence, at just the right speed, with a specific job for everybody in the room. But I learned, and in time I came to love the briefing; I've come to appreciate just how important a good brief can be to a successful corporate mission, and I believe most of my seminar attendees would say the same thing. Add briefings to your company's regular regimen, and you may find yourself both gratified by your bottom line and thanked by your employees.

SUMMARY

The rubber meets the road at the mission briefing. That's where the combat mission plan is transformed into specific actions assigned to specific people at specific times. It is the fighter pilot community's version of a business planning meeting, except that its form is more prescribed, its elements are more procedural and detailed, and its tone is more serious. This is where the life-and-death details are communicated.

A good understanding of the proper elements of a military-style mission briefing can improve anyone's leadership of those important gatherings where truly important plans are made.

The backbone of a good mission brief is preparation. Moreover, the leader has to be *demonstrably, extensively* prepared, so that the cumulative effect of the preparation elicits commitment among the participants. In setting up the briefing, follow these guidelines:

1. Set the time, place, and duration of the briefing, and do not vary from these settings.

2. Have all whiteboard and visual elements prepared, with backups for all electrical and mechanical devices.

3. State the mission objective—a clear and achievable goal.

4. Establish a time hack—a set of time parameters for the mission.

5. Brief the environment of the mission—the physical and attitudinal factors that will have an impact on the outcome.

6. Brief the mission standards—the "motherhood," in pilot talk—and the contingencies arising from them.

7. Brief the nature of the threat, as thoroughly as possible.

8. Brief the tactics selected to accomplish the mission objective, concentrating on the decision matrix that will serve as your team's guide to contingencies and action.

9. Just like in planning, always—always—brief the contingencies.

8

THE ART OF EXECUTION

Ask a fighter pilot how to execute a mission and you'll probably be greeted by a puzzled look. You might as well be asking him what color white is, or what love is. To a fighter pilot, the brief *is* the execution, and the execution is the brief; they're one and the same. Remember, a good brief covers everything he does from the moment he steps to the jet to the moment he walks back into the squadron building for the debrief. A fighter pilot simply executes the brief: end of story.

But that's not to say pilots haven't developed some helpful skills to get through a mission. They have. And they very much apply to your business mission.

IDENTIFY YOUR MISSION-CRITICAL COMPONENTS AND FOCUS ON THEM AS YOU EXECUTE

Fighter combat missions are complex. Often too complex, in fact. They involve literally hundreds of sequential actions, countless variables, endless contingencies, and threats too numerous to mention. Fighter pilots have learned that the trick to managing all of it is not to improve their brainpower to Mensa levels, but to *simplify*. No matter what your mission, your timetable, or the unique risk factors of your mission, simplifying is an absolute necessity as you progress through the timeline of a mission.

The first step to simplification is to *identify your mission-critical components*—and stay on top of them no matter what else happens.

Within every briefing are critical events or conditions that must be monitored in all circumstances, from the time the mission begins until its successful conclusion. These are absolutes—the things that, even when all else fails, must be accomplished for mission success and survival. Keeping the mission-critical components foremost in your mind will help make decisions easier when you find yourself faced with one of the countless variables that weren't (or couldn't be) briefed. Let me give you an example.

I can screw up a lot of things in my F–15, but one thing I don't ever want to do is lose track of the distance between me and my adversary—my *distance to target*. Distance to target is a mission-critical component. Every radio call I get from AWACs includes an updated distance to target; every function on my aircraft depends on that number. All my weapons have ranges. If I lose track of where I am, or if I lose track of my distance to target, I may slip inside the enemy's weapons envelope and suddenly find myself with a missile turning toward my engines. If I get in too close, my missiles are no good; if I lose track of that and don't switch to guns, I'll soon be bailing out of a bullet-ridden F–15. Distance to target means everything to me. Even if other aspects of the mission have gone awry—bad radio communication, poor formation flying—I'll still be viable if I keep my awareness of the distance to target.

Distance to target is very specific to my unique mission—air-to-air combat—just as your mission-critical component should be very specific to your company and your unique mission. NASA, for example, is in many ways the paragon of an execution-oriented organization. It deals in complex systems, often with precious human cargo aboard. For NASA the mission-critical component is always *100 percent safety*. If any system isn't a go, the countdown stops. Each and every measure taken during the countdown relates in some way to the safe execution of the mission. If anything falls outside the tight parameters of a NASA launch, the countdown stops until the problem is identified and fixed.

For most businesses, of course, stopping the countdown is unrealistic—and for some the mission-critical component is exactly the opposite. Take the high-risk world of the Broadway theater, which has one of the most famous mission-critical components ever devised: *The show must go on.* On Broadway, punctuality is paramount—no matter what or who is involved. If the leading lady is ill, there's a fail-safe contingency plan in the form of an understudy waiting to take over the role. If someone misses a line, if a set falls down—the show goes on. They may sound like an unlikely pair of professions to match up, but theater casts and crews have much in common with fighter pilot squadrons: Each group rehearses and plans for dozens of what-ifs and contingencies so that when it's showtime there are as few surprises as possible.

Believe it or not, even something as intangible as *feel* can be a mission-critical component—in the right circumstances. Case in point: the Ben Hogan Company. Mr. Hogan was perhaps the most admired and talented professional golfer ever to grace the PGA tour, but he was also an exacting taskmaster. When he started the Ben Hogan Company, he set out to make clubs with unmatched feel and control. The day those first thousand or so irons were delivered to him for his inspection, he thought his dream had come true. Every dollar of equity capital he and his partner had was invested in those sets. There they were, ready for the market. But they were never sold. Those Ben Hogan irons failed to satisfy their mission-critical component—they didn't *feel* right. When Mr. Hogan powered a bucket of balls off the tee, he said, the feel was wrong. Instead of putting an inferior product on the market (and despite the devastating impact to his profit-and-loss), he ordered the heads sawed off and the clubs rebuilt.

I learned about the mission-critical components early in my business life—and I learned the hard way. I had just been promoted to sales manager for Triple M. The sales department was not in good shape, and now that I was sales manager, I was going to clean house. That was my mission—to beef up our sales force. So I fired all of them but one, and started looking for the kind of leaning-forward, hard-charging salespeople that would take us into the next decade. Days, then weeks went by, and I had no qualified candidates.

One day, in the midst of it all, my uncle, the president of the company, came to see me. Up to now he'd shown no alarm, hadn't interfered with my new sales plan in the least. But on this day, he had questions. I told him what I'd done and outlined my vision for the future. He said, "That's great. I hope it works out." He turned to leave, then stopped and said, "Oh, by the way, you *are* going to meet your sales quota this month, aren't you?" My jaw went slack! I had forgotten Triple M's mission-critical component—*sales*, and specifically a monthly quota that was crucial to the company's bottom line. It really wasn't a question, of course. He didn't care what I had to do, he just needed his sales quota met. Needless to say, I had a very busy month.

Any good salesperson would say that his *only* mission-critical component is *selling*. But that's too broad a statement for a whole sales department. Here's a better one that one client of ours has instituted: Each rep must make no fewer than *five* face-to-face sales calls per day. That's what salespeople do for TDI, the outdoor advertising firm, the one that requires its employees to wear the company pin on their lapels. They feel that at least five sales calls a day will make them successful. And so far they've been right. Today TDI is one of the fastest-growing divisions of CBS, Inc.

What is the mission-critical component for your business? Do what we fighter pilots do. Even in the heat of everyday business, know it and keep it foremost in your mind. If you do, it will allow you to make correct choices even when unexpected, unbriefed events threaten to derail the mission.

CLOSE DOWN THE CLUTTER

Every fighter pilot does this. It's not something that's taught as much as something that's learned. It's about simplifying and freeing up your mind to handle what needs to be handled *now*, as you execute. Let me use a computer analogy: Consider the difference between random access memory (RAM), which processes data quickly but is limited in size, and the hard drive, which processes data more slowly but is almost unlimited in size. As humans we keep a lot of things open in RAM, but at some point you run out of RAM just as you do on a computer, and the elements start to get jumbled; if things get really overloaded, the computer might even shut down. When that happens, you have only one choice: Move stuff to the hard drive to make room. We do this in flying; we call it *closing down,* and it's an incredibly valuable habit to remember as you execute, particularly in more demanding or complex missions.

Let's say it's the morning of a big mission. I have to fly a one-v.-one at a military range 100 miles north of our base. It so happens that things are a mess at my house—there are bills to pay, the repairman is coming, and my girlfriend is mad at me for forgetting her birthday. I'll deal with all that with complete focus (especially the apologies to my girlfriend!), but the minute I walk out the door and head toward the base, I throw a mental firewall between the home front and my flying. I dump the home issues down onto my hard drive—and that's where they'll stay until I'm back that night.

Once out of the house, I open the car door, get in, maneuver through the morning traffic, get frustrated with the lousy drivers, and ultimately get to the base and park. I get out, slam the door shut—and with it I close down the car and the traffic and the congestion in my mind. Car? What car?

Next I get my flight suit on and walk into the briefing room. I go through the mission, brief each contingency, write down what I need to know on my line-up card, and out we go to the jets. As the squadron room door swings shut behind me, the day-in, day-out world of the squadron closes down, too. Now I'm thinking about jets.

On and on it goes. As I walk up to the jet I do my preflight inspection, but as I climb the ladder, grab the canopy rails, and lower myself into the seat, I bury everything in the hard drive but the inside of that cockpit. Now I'm focused on the mission. Now I'm looking ahead. My mind is fresh, free, undistracted, ready to turn and burn.

Closing down is nothing more than a mental tactic that puts you totally "in the moment"—that is, in the present, without the burden of the past or the worries of the future to make things complicated. It forces you to direct your energies toward the mission at hand—the only way to fly.

SHIFTING YOUR FOCUS FORWARD

We do many things during a mission. We taxi, take off, air refuel, handle our weapons and radar, refuel again, and land. But we don't do it all at once. One of the tricks of the trade we fighter pilots use is called *shifting your focus forward*—a strategy that allows us to move from task to task efficiently and safely.

Let me explain by using an air refueling scenario. Air refueling is one of the most interesting things we do as pilots. At 25,000 feet above the ground, we fly our jets to within a dozen feet of a giant KC–10 tanker—essentially a three-engined flying gas station—and get gas. We call it *hanging on the boom*. We're both traveling at 310 knots. We may be in a banked turn; often we're in and out of the clouds.

The procedure looks dangerous, because we're so close, but it's actually one of the safest things we do. It does, though, involve a few things that I don't do during any other part of my mission. For instance, as I get close to the tanker, I have to watch a pattern of red and green lights on the underside of the KC–10 to help me line up for the refueling. On the radio, I talk to the boom operator as he works the nozzle into the receptacle. I pay close attention to precise formation flying, because we are only twelve feet apart. But just as soon as the boom releases, I'm finished refueling and I cross refueling off my to-do list. *I shift my focus forward to the next event.* If we're going to the gunnery range, I can start thinking about my weapons switchology, the pattern I'll fly against my opponent, and the what-ifs of air-to-air gunnery. I don't have to think about air refueling anymore; that's behind me.

That's not to say that I forget about refueling altogether. Quite the opposite: I don't bury this in the hard drive. This is where shifting focus differs from closing down. When I shift focus, I keep air refueling open in my mental RAM; I may have a sudden emergency and need to get back on the boom ASAP—I just don't need to think about it right now. It stays open in my RAM because if I do have an emergency, I won't have the time to think about how to fly the boom and what my closure procedures are; I'll just have to do it. So I don't close that program down the way I do with my domestic issues. I just shift my focus forward and allow my mind to concentrate on the next portion of the mission.

LISTEN MORE, TALK LESS

Pilots quickly learn the value and necessity of listening more and talking less. Our airwaves are always crowded, and no one needs a chatty pilot using a dozen words when five would do. In fact, pilots take great pride in using efficient, confident, abbreviated communication.

The flip side to efficient talking is good listening. Listening is critical to both situational awareness and good execution. Fighter pilots use their ears almost as much as their eyes; there are all sorts of coded audio tones and signals for which we're always listening. For instance, one audio signal tells me when enemy radar is locating my jet, while a very different audible warns me that the enemy pilot has chosen to lock me up, which usually means he's about to fire a missile at me. Then there are the controllers: I need to keep an ear out for my call sign popping up in that blur of message traffic. Controllers are pros at brief, efficient communication. Out of the blue I may hear, "Cheetah One One, snap zero eight zero." How easy it would be to miss those seven words—but if I did, I'd probably be dead. "Snap" is a trigger word we use to mean *heads up right now!*, such as when a mid-air collision is imminent or a missile is on my tail. "Snap zero eight zero" means to turn to a heading of 080 degrees *immediately*. Can you imagine *not* paying attention in a fighter jet?

That's why we're always listening, particularly during the executional phase. Similarly, communications clutter in business situations creates a cacophony that complicates the environment needlessly. Good listening and short, efficient verbalizing help keep the mission swift and efficient—and ensure that you don't miss important information.

WHEN-AND-IF-ING

Throughout the execution phases of our mission, pilots are always "when-and-if-ing." That's the first thing we do when we shift our focus forward to the next stage of the mission. When I shift my focus forward to air refueling, my thoughts immediately turn to a set of familiar cause-and-effect scenarios: "When the boom misses the intake valve and smashes out my cockpit glass, I'm going to lean forward and descend." Or, "If I can't connect, I'll drop off and regroup for ten seconds." In other words, I actively anticipate the bad things that can happen so that I'm ready to act if they do. This kind of proactive anticipation process eliminates the shock of surprise, and saves a few precious seconds of time if something really does go wrong. "When the engine catches fire, I'll pull the ejection seat handles." "When the engine flames out, I'll go through the restart procedures." "When a landing gear light doesn't come on, I'll recycle the gear." "When I get on target as briefed, we'll split the CAP into lanes"—and so on.

When-and-if-ing can be valuable in a wide variety of business situations. As your partner is presenting the new product data to the buyer, are you when-and-if-ing the buyer's likely objections? On payday, if the lines at the bank teller windows reach the door, as a manager are you prepared to open a new window? When you run out of the giveaway items at the store opening, do you have a plan to round up more quickly?

When-and-if-ing means moving forward *prepared*, all the way, all the time. I've already stated that flexibility is the key to air power. Here's the collary: Preparation is the key to flexibility.

KNOW WHEN TO ABORT

My mission is air-to-air combat, but sometimes we "blow through" the engagement and hightail it home. For dozens of tactical reasons, a flight lead might decide that the formation is in a disadvantageous position, and that it would be better to bug out than to turn and engage. If we're going beak to beak, closing at 1,000 miles per hour, and we run into problems that could cost us a jet, we'll just blow through the enemy formation and speed out of the area. In most cases, we'll regroup and reengage, but in a low-risk situation, we're not going to commit suicide. Knowing when to turn and fight and when to bug out is a coldly tactical execution skill.

Where does this skill most apply in the business world? Clearly, in new product development. Marketers and other operations people need to hone their skills to the point that they recognize an unwinnable fight, and save their execution assets for engagements they can win. For example, every ten years or so some new marketing manager in the distilled spirits industry tries to push the introduction of a clear bourbon. It's an understandable idea; it makes a clear competitive statement, and after all the brown is only the result of coloring. But consumers have consistently voted with their dollars that they only want a traditional, brown-colored bourbon. Distillers have so far wisely decided not to spend a lot of money to change their minds.

You'll probably remember the "New Coke" fiasco. In the 1980s, responding to inroads made by rival Pepsi, Coke's new product people rolled out a new, reformulated Coke with a sweeter taste. The response from consumers was overwhelmingly negative. Instead of pushing the brand forward, Coke abandoned the new product immediately, and restored their flagship brand under the banner "Classic Coke."

PERSONALIZE AS MANY OF THE ASPECTS OF A MISSION AS YOU CAN

Ultimately, what is it that makes for successful execution? Isn't it a feeling of personal responsibility, an overriding personal interest in a successful outcome? If my pilots don't really care whether our mission is successful, no amount of planning and empowerment will help us win. So how do you make someone care about the outcome? One answer, I believe, is in instilling employees with a sense of mission, and a feeling of personal value to the successful outcome of the mission. It's something I've alluded to throughout this book, and it's something that we do in the fighter pilot community. But let me give you an example that illustrates how personalizing the mission has worked in business. A friend of mine acquired a concrete company. Sales were fine, but morale among the concrete truck drivers seemed to be low, and the amount of equipment breakdown was intolerable—and clearly due to the fact that no one seemed to care about anything more than going home at the end of the day. Execution was, to say the least, lazy.

Frustrated by how ineffective all his remedies were, my friend tried something a little different. He took a chapter out of the fighter pilot book of experience, and made each driver the "commander" of his own truck. No one else could touch his vehicle. The driver's name was painted on the side. Elaborate paint jobs, in the manner of World War II "nose art," were added to each truck. Maintenance of each vehicle became the responsibility of the driver. In short, he personalized the execution of the mission. It wasn't a company truck hauling cement; it was Joe's truck. It wasn't a company truck broken down on the side of the road; it was Mike's truck.

In a very short period of time, morale went sky-high, maintenance problems virtually disappeared, and business was going smoothly. What had changed? The drivers felt a new sense of ownership and involvement; they'd been shown that the company trusted them and valued them—that they were individuals with names, not just "the drivers"—and together they made a team, and a distinctive, colorful one at that. This made all the difference in the world, and it paid out in the most important part of the operation—the execution of the basic mission.

SUMMARY

Executing a mission plan is a simple matter of performing tasks sequentially, as outlined in the combat mission brief. First I do this, second I do this, and so on, all the way to completion. But there are a few things pilots do to sharpen their execution skills, and all of them can be very helpful to anyone in the midst of executing his own mission:

1. Maintain focus by establishing the mission-critical component. What is the one objective that *must* be accomplished on your mission, no matter what? Whatever it is, that's your *mission-critical component.* When execution is jeopardized by unexpected events, keep it in mind. Nothing else matters as long as the mission-critical component is accomplished.

2. Simplify by closing down the clutter. Closing down areas of your life that are not directly pertinent to the mission at hand is a mental management technique. It is a way of staying focused in the present, without distractions.

3. Move your focus forward. All missions move forward in stages. As each stage is accomplished, cross it off your list and shift your focus ahead to the next stage. Don't look back!

4. Listen, don't talk. Execution efficiency can be compromised by too many voices fighting for attention. Keep the noise level down. There may be warning signals going off, and you don't want to miss them.

5. Know when to abort. Sometimes the best execution is *not* to execute. When all the signs tell you that a fight will only get you killed, back off. Fall back and find another time and another place to plant the flag.

6. "When-and-if" every phase of the mission. Save yourself precious time by anticipating as much as possible. We've talked about the contingencies of every phase of the mission. Be prepared for both good and bad things to happen. Remember, the key to air power is flexibility—and you can't be flexible if you're not prepared.

7. Establish a sense of value to the mission. Nothing inspires execution more than a shared understanding of the importance of the mission and its members. The more you can help your team members become emotionally invested in the mission, the better your outcome is likely to be.

9

TASK SATURATION: THE OBSTACLE
TO FLAWLESS EXECUTION

We all knew what caused it the moment we saw the fighter jet crash in the desert. We didn't know the exact details, but the short film clip pretty much said it all. A military fighter pilot was coming into a gunnery range for a strafing run on a target. He was flying the jet with the typical turns and banks we use to roll in on a target. He was coming in low, transiting into the target area, then began a steep climb to visually acquire the target—the pop before the attack. Once he had the target, he rolled the jet back down, pointed his nose at it, and locked it up. Down the chute he went, descending, getting ever faster, 500 miles per hour, making his radio calls, homing in on the bull's-eye on the desert floor. His right hand on the stick, his left on the throttle, his index finger putting pressure on the trigger as he came closer and closer—the run was on.

I can't tell you the precise moment when we all knew something was wrong, but every fighter pilot in the room instinctively tensed up as the jet dipped a little too close to the ground. We expected the pilot to correct the problem, but it never happened. Sure enough—wham!—the jet crashed into the ground and exploded in a ball of flaming JP–4 fuel.

We watched in silence as the smoke rose into the sky. Then we heard our instructor pilot speak. "Gentlemen," he said, "what you just saw was a classic case of task saturation."

In the fighter pilot community we strive for a mistake-free world. The preflight brief discussed in Chapter 7 is designed to enhance execution to the point that mistakes are eliminated. Yet mistakes get made. Why? The only answer is that we're all human, and none of us is infallible. For fighter pilots, the most obvious evidence of that is our seeming obsession with the contingencies phase of the brief— we're all too aware of the mistakes even the best of us can make.

But rather than throw up our hands and resign ourselves to the laws of probability and fate, we in the Air Force have, over the course of time, tried to find a pattern to our errors, to learn from our mistakes, to reduce or eliminate as many of them as we can. That's why we never sweep our accidents under the rug. That's why we view gruesome footage of accidents when they happen. We call crashes *lessons learned.* Each accident helps us find ways to prevent them in the future.

After years of scrutiny, we believe we have isolated the root cause of about 75 percent of our mistakes. We call it the *silent killer*—task saturation.

OVERLOAD

As I stated earlier, you and I live in very similar environments. Like the blur of air-to-air combat, today's business environment is a spinning, topsy-turvy world of people demanding that you do more with less—less time and fewer assets. Look at your average day: It's only 9 A.M., but your cell phone just went off for the fifteenth time. Your beeper is ringing. You're trying to wade through the twenty e-mails you got overnight. You have a call report to write. Your spouse phones to say the car is ready at the shop, but it needs to be picked up by noon. Your assistant walks in and says that a trusted vendor is outside and has to see you right away. Your boss walks in and says he needs a report on his desk by four o'clock that afternoon. The phone rings. And rings, and rings, and rings. Before you know it, you're maxed-out. Your mission is failing. You can't do another thing or think another thought. You can't even remember what you were supposed to do. Noon comes and goes, and around three o'clock you remember . . . *the car!*

Wham! Your jet just hit the ground.

Fighter pilots know the deadly trap of task saturation. In fact, in the early years, when the first jet fighters were being designed and developed, one of the biggest obstacles the Air Force faced was how to help pilots cope with the daunting task of trying to handle a single-seat craft all alone. How could one person monitor all the gauges, fly the airplane at breakneck speeds, and employ the weapons simultaneously, especially in air combat? It was a question that transcended ordinary ergonomics and physical capacity. It had to do with *processing* power—brain power. Could the human brain stay ahead of the machine? How much cognitive work could a human being accomplish while being bombarded with multiple data streams, multiple sensory stimuli, uncomfortable and distracting body pressures in the nine-G range, vertigo, and the claustrophobia of an oxygen mask?

What they found should come as no surprise. At a certain point, pilots became task-overloaded, and when that occurred, the ability to perform both cognitive and mechanical tasks declined drastically. Further, they found that this task-saturated state was insidious—that is, *the pilot wasn't aware of its onset*.

The results were usually the same—the pilot tended to lose control of his aircraft without even knowing it was happening. All of us in the fighter pilot community know of aviators who flew perfectly good jets into the ground, and probably didn't know they were doing it until the end.

In the fighter pilot community we call this *dying relaxed*. You can call it the exact same thing, because it has the same effect on you as it does on me—the briefing is out the window, execution is nil, task saturation brings your job to a halt, and your mission fails.

TASK SATURATION: THE SYMPTOMS

In our seminars, we ask our audience if they've ever felt task-saturated. Without fail, all hands go up. Then we ask, "How does task saturation show itself?" Put another way, what are the symptoms of task saturation? The question usually brings a hush over the room. Nobody is quite sure what his symptoms are, although every so often someone will venture that the onset of stress is a good indication.

Stress is, in fact, a likely sign of task saturation. But there are other, more specific symptoms, and you should be aware of them. In our Air Force training, we're taught to be alert to three human responses to task saturation. These responses are *shutdown*, *compartmentalization*, and *channelization*. And, unless you're very lucky, you can find them all in your business world too.

Shutdown

Faced with an overwhelming volume of tasks, some people simply quit working. I'm sure you've either seen it or experienced it yourself: They walk outside, go to the health club, take an early lunch; they go home and hide. In one form or the other, they abandon their work because they see no way to complete it. They simply turn off.

Interestingly, psychologists say this is an appropriate response under some circumstances. An avalanche of overwork for a long duration can cause depression, nervous breakdowns, and physical problems, including heart attacks. Any perceptive boss who sees such symptoms in an employee would immediately advise a few days away from the office, perhaps even to see a doctor.

But most task saturation situations are momentary, not long-term, and rarely do they end requiring drastic responses such as leaves of absence or medical attention. Nonetheless, an employee with no energy—one who is listless, depressed, and stares off into the distance; who takes repeated breaks, wanders off for long lunches, or engages in meaningless but lengthy conversations—is very likely an employee who has shut down out of task saturation. The only sure remedy is to reduce his workload, perhaps even reduce his responsibilities. If it's a temporary situation, the employee should bounce back, and the problem will be over. But even minor appearances of task saturation need to be recognized, for however fleeting they may be, they constitute an obstacle to your mission.

Compartmentalizing

Compartmentalizing is another symptom of task saturation. Compartmentalizers try to cope with their overload by dividing their tasks into boxes and concentrating on them one at a time. They're endeavoring to create a mental filing system, a way of cutting their burdens down to size and making them manageable. Again, this may sound sensible—but compartmentalization is essentially a linear way of thinking, as opposed to an integrated or comprehensive approach, and relies for its success on moving from one box to another in a sequential fashion. It's also, in a sense, a dangerous form of gambling.

The danger of compartmentalizing lies in the temptation to relax those areas of the brain that aren't directly engaged. For instance, on a B–52 there are eight engines, each with four or five gauges on the instrument panel, which means that the pilot has forty or so engine gauges to monitor. If a B–52 pilot gets task-saturated, he might compartmentalize and focus just on the engines—gambling, in essence, that other tasks (such as navigation or even basic pilotage) will take care of themselves until he can return to focusing on them exclusively once again.

For a fighter pilot rushing into the merge, compartmentalizing might mean shutting down the tactical portion of the brain to concentrate on formation flying. Trapped into this kind of sequential thinking, that same pilot might then turn from his formation to his weapons, then to his altitude; if anything should go wrong in one area while he's devoting all his attention to another—and things can go wrong in this environment in a matter of milliseconds—he runs a real risk of flying right into the ground.

It's important to distinguish between compartmentalization and the kind of focus-shifting tactic we discussed in the last chapter. What pilots should develop is the ability to stay alert to all the basic elements of their environment—to keep several files open in

RAM, as we said, while focusing on one. What they need to guard against is that moment when the brain says, *I need to relax a little bit*—when task saturation begins to set in. When that happens the pilot's deeply ingrained habit of constant box-to-box monitoring can begin to fade—and ultimately disappear altogether. Sooner or later the compartmentalized brain is pushing away new information, misjudging its priority, and refusing to stay as flexible as the situation warrants.

Let me give you an example.

You're flying along at Red Flag, one of the largest air-to-air combat exercises we fly; 120 jet aircraft are airborne at one time. You're escorting a sixty-aircraft strike package into a target. You're twenty miles ahead of the package leading an eight-ship of F–15s, and you're the eight-ship leader. Your job is to eliminate any airborne threats so the strikers can drop bombs on their targets. There's obviously a lot of communication going on. You're trying to fly good formation, and you're trying to do it using a bare minimum of communication because there are a lot of voices on the radio right now. But you've got to make sure you find a way to tell your wingman whom to target and what to do. You're also flying low, because the strikers today are low, so you've got to think about evading enemy radar. At 700 miles an hour, flying low gives you no margin for error.

All of a sudden the combat controller—let's call him Darkstar— says, "Engage target on your nose at thirty miles." So, *wham!* you go from a strategic mindset to a tactical mindset, and you start locking on to the target, identifying it as friend or foe, and talking to your wingmen to prioritize who's shooting who and how. Now here's where compartmentalization occurs: In the middle of this, in the heat of battle, you don't hear the warning beeps of an air-to-air aircraft locking on to you. You're supposed to respond to the beep, to direct your eyes to the radar warning scope, but you don't. You're so caught up with your target lock you don't hear anything at all. You're compartmentalized. Your brain is focused on the target ahead and the ground rushing by below. You've actually shut out the part of your brain that responds to audibles.

All of a sudden, Darkstar comes on and says, "Cheetah, snap 270 degrees"—and you don't hear that call either. Remember, the word "snap" for a fighter pilot means *Drop everything you're doing now and turn this direction immediately*, because they're seeing something dangerous that you're not seeing. For example, there's an untargeted threat at your six o'clock and you'd better take some evasive action or somebody is going to shoot a missile up your tailpipe. Instead of snapping to 270, you make a radio call to your wingman, "Engage nose twenty miles, 15,000 feet, Fox Three." That means that you've launched your AMRAAM missile at the targets and you're focusing everything you can on making sure that this one missile hits the target because, of course, you're compartmentalized. A couple of seconds go by, and everyone else in the war has heard it but you—"Cheetah, *snap* 270 degrees." Warnings and beeps are going off and you're not hearing any of it.

Electronically, you just got killed.

Later on at the debrief you'll be the feature act in the highlight reel.

That's compartmentalized attention—or, as you might also think of it, that's a death wish.

Channelizing

Channelizing is the act of focusing attention on one particular thing to the exclusion of all other things. Channelizing is compartmentalizing to the extreme. Instead of not hearing radio calls, as our first pilot failed to do, the channelizer would shut down *all* his cognitive faculties and would not only not hear anything but would likely lose even his basic flying skills for the sake of keeping the radar lock. Channelizers get into tiny feedback loops; they focus on *single* instruments or on a small, individual problem at the expense of everything else.

In that chaotic office scenario cited above, where the boss said he needed a report by four o'clock, a channelizer would respond by turning off his beeper, taking his phone off the hook, telling his assistant to lock the door and admit no one, and telling his wife he can't pick up the car—he's got a report to do. World War III might break out in the street, and he'd have no idea.

In the short term, nothing disastrous might happen while the channelizer bunkers in; but the method makes him (and the entire office) vulnerable to a whole range of fast-breaking problems that might need fast solutions. But it's not just a bad work habit; if a company channelizes the entire business could collapse.

For pilots, channelizing is a problem that has serious consequences. Twenty-eight years ago an airliner crashed as the result of channelized attention. You may remember it—Eastern Flight 401. Three experienced pilots and ninety-six passengers died.

Eastern 401 was a Lockheed L–1011, one of the most sophisticated commercial airliners in the sky. It was the newest of the new generation of wide-bodied airplanes and it had both state-of-the-art electronics and all the creature comforts a pilot or passenger could want. This L–1011, however, was bound for tragedy.

We'll pick up the story at the end of the flight. Based on the NTSB report, the L–1011, en route to Miami, was on its ten-mile final approach to Miami International Airport, 2,000 feet above sea level, and on a normal descent for the landing. It was a dark night, but perfectly clear, with no weather problems whatsoever.

The first officer, who was at the controls, turned to the captain and said, "Gear down, before-landing checklist." Standard procedure: the FO was calling for the landing gear and then the checklist. The captain threw the gear handle down and then waited for the three green lights to come on the panel indicating that the nose gear and the two main gears were down and locked.

There was a pause, as there always is, as the gear traveled down. The crew waited for the three greens. But they didn't get them. Only *two* greens came on. The left and right main gear lights were on, but the nose gear light was not illuminated. That appeared to mean that the nose gear had not come down, but that was such an unusual thing that the crew had to consider other problems, too. Could it be a bad light bulb? A bad relay? Or had the nose gear really failed?

The captain pulled out the emergency landing gear checklist, which told him to cycle the gear handle again. He did so. Still two greens. The captain then said, "It's probably a burned-out light bulb. Let's test it." So the first officer pushed it in to reseat it, but no luck; it still failed to illuminate. So they reasoned that they had a bad bulb. The captain then said to the first officer, "Put this damn thing on autopilot and let's figure out why this light won't go on." All three men put their heads into fixing the light bulb.

It is important to make note of the autopilot. Probably 90 percent of commercial flights are on autopilot at 2,000 feet. But when a plane is on autopilot, it is still the flying pilot's responsibility to monitor the status of the aircraft continually. In this case, the flying pilot was the first officer, who sat in the right seat.

Then the fatal problem crept up. As the first officer leaned forward to help pry the bulb from its mount, he exerted a small pressure on the yoke. The Lockheed L–1011 autopilot is designed so that when a push or pull force greater than a few pounds is exerted against the control wheel, the aircraft says to itself, "Hey, I think the pilot wants to fly the airplane." *Click*, the autopilot disengaged. When it did, the L–1011 began a gentle, slow descent, imperceptible to anyone, free-flying toward the marshes below.

At night over water with a dark sky, the sky and the water tend to blend together to disguise the horizon. No one in the cabin had a clue that the plane was descending. And the pilots, focused on the little bulb, were channelized to the max. As they flew through 1,500 feet, the air traffic controller, who probably noticed the unusual descent, came on the radio, saying, "Eastern 401, how are things going out there?" But Eastern 401 was so channelized that, while they heard the radio call, they didn't really *listen* to it. They answered perfunctorily, "Uh, Roger Eastern 401," and clicked off the mike. The controller, for some reason assured by this answer, shifted his attention to other traffic. Seconds went by.

With just 120 feet above ground showing on the altimeter, the first officer finally came up for air. He looked at the altimeter and didn't believe what he was seeing. One hundred twenty feet! He was supposed to be at 2,000 feet! The first officer asked, "We're at 2,000 feet, right?" A few precious seconds were lost as his cognitive functions spun back into gear. Perhaps the first officer was trying to reconcile what the altimeter said and what he believed should be true—that the airplane was at 2,000 feet. For the next twelve seconds, no one reacted to the altimeter.

Could the aircraft have been saved at this point? The experts think so. Push the throttles up, pull back on the control wheel, and fly to safety. But the correction had to be made immediately. The National Traffic Safety Board re-creation of the crash shows that the Eastern 401 crew did not react immediately. Why? The cockpit voice recorder reveals that the crew spent the next twelve seconds—the rest of their lives—trying to figure out what *had* happened instead of reacting to what *was* happening in the very urgent present. Down they went, the altimeter reading out the fatal numbers: a hundred feet . . . fifty feet . . . twenty feet . . . boom. Ninety-nine people died because three experienced professional pilots forgot to fly the plane while they channelized on a twenty-cent light bulb.

IDENTIFYING TASK SATURATION IN YOUR LIFE

Every human has the ability to cope with different levels of task saturation. Some people can handle more than others. The most important thing is to identify the effect it has on you and to be prepared to react to it. When I get task-saturated, for example, my radio comm gets lax. I start missing radio calls, or I start checking in late, or I start using words that aren't standard fighter pilot language. I just don't sound cool and calm on the radio anymore, and that's one of my most important assignments. Pilot communications have to be short and concise, to convey the maximum amount of information in a minimum amount of time. Sounding controlled and commanding is part of my job as flight lead. Even when I'm pulling nine G's, checking six, upside-down, and inhaling and exhaling very deeply, I get it all together and make a nice, clean, smooth radio call. When I start getting sloppy with my radio comm, I know I'm starting to get task-saturated.

Task saturation is so common among pilots that we actually include it in our briefings; it's part of the contingencies in motherhood. "Task saturation is going to be a player in this mission." Night vision goggles, which can have the effect of distancing pilots from their sense of reality, sometimes exacerbate the problem, so at the briefing we'll try to warn the pilots in advance of the danger. "If you start getting overloaded, take your goggles off. Revert to your old instrument scan. Get your brain back flying the aircraft. Get yourself oriented."

But even without night vision goggles, task saturation can occur. My rule with my wingman is this: If he gets task-saturated, I want him to fall out of the tactical mindset for a minute and get himself together. He can bug out to a safe area until he feels comfortable again, then come back and rejoin the formation. After that he can get back into the tactical aspects of the mission. It is the air combat equivalent of getting up from your desk and walking around to clear your head.

Sometimes, though, it isn't that simple; sometimes time is precious, and things get complicated. If I get the sense that my wingman is so task-saturated that he's on the verge of going *tango uniform* (brain dead), then I have to take other action. I'd rather not jeopardize the mission by losing his eight weapons, so I'll tell him to fall back to the basics of formation flying and stand down with the other responsibilities. I'll let him get in position and get his formation flying fixed first, and then I'll gradually start getting him back up to speed, doing what I can to bolster his situational awareness and return him to the loop. I'll say, "Okay, here's where we are, Two, we're twenty-two miles from the threat. We have two groups [formations] in a north-south split. One is at 15,000, the other is at 20,000. I want you to lock the southern group at 20,000; that's your job. Any questions, Two?"

"Nope."

Okay, then he's back up to speed, and we can all get back to the tactical execution of the mission.

If that doesn't work, I'll probably hear him say, "Two is tumbleweeds." That's the call that says, *I'm definitely task-saturated*. It's a cry for help: *I don't know where we are, I don't know what we're doing*. It tells me that that pilot is going to be no help at all, other than that he's flying along with us. In those cases, if we're far enough away from the threat, I'll try turning the formation "cold." I'm going to say, "Okay, Cheetah 180 left." We'll get away from the threat for a while and I'll try to get the pilot back on track, tell him what's going on, and get him up to speed. When he's back on track I'll say, "Cheetah turn 180 hot," and we'll all reengage the threat.

BUSINESS REMEDIES

As we've seen, the business environment has become so fast-paced and task-saturated that you and everyone you work with are at risk of suffering the debilitating effects of task saturation. Once the problem is brought to their attention, almost all our seminar attendees are able to identify their own symptoms of task saturation and then think through a personal trick to cope with it. What are your personal indicators of task saturation? Not going through your e-mails daily? Not responding to telephone calls?

And what's your most common type of task saturation? Compartmentalizing, channelizing, or shutting down? Try to identify the point at which you are task-saturated, and then think through some remedies that you can put into effect today. Do it with your group and see if you can find group indicators of task saturation. Don't worry if the solutions don't come easy—some of the tips in the next chapter may be just what you need.

SUMMARY

No amount of preparation or training will eliminate mistakes. The human factor always enters the equation, and human performance is fallible. But rather than simply accept this fact, the fighter pilot community studies it, hoping to reduce the human risk factors in the cockpit. By far the biggest cause of pilot error is the stress-based paralysis known as task saturation: too many things to do in too short a time.

Task saturation is not a condition limited to fighter pilots. Daily business life (some would say *all* of American life) is becoming more task-saturated every day. There can be deadly consequences to task saturation, because the mind can respond in three damaging ways:

1. It can **shut down**—that is, turn itself off as a way of fleeing what it perceives to be an impossible situation.

2. It can **compartmentalize**—that is, shut down certain parts of the brain as a way of focusing all resources on a narrow course of action or thought. The danger lies in the fact that the mind does not carry out its overview function while it is compartmentalized.

3. It can **channelize**—that is, focus on one thing only, to the exclusion of all other data, sensory stimuli, or thought.

The onset of task saturation is subtle, and its effects are insidious. For that reason it is important to self-diagnose, and identify when you are reaching the task saturation point.

10

OVERCOMING TASK SATURATION

It was a night intercept mission. I was fighting another F–15 a hundred miles off the coast of Georgia, and there was bad weather all around. As we hunted each other down, I had to maneuver between towering thunderheads and scattered clouds. Even at 30,000 feet, I could make out the whitecaps blowing off the waves across the ocean below.

Weather aside, this was one of those darker-than-dark nights. Few stars were in sight between the layers of clouds. My gauges glowed brightly against this blanket of black, but even with the familiar dials and instruments, I felt terribly alone. Being in a jet fighter a hundred miles from land can make you feel pretty small.

I was checking my radar for the bogey when all hell broke loose in my cockpit. Red warning lights blazed to life. My yellow master caution started flashing. Over my headphones I heard Bitchin' Betty, the cockpit voice prompter, saying, "Warning! Warning! FTIT over temp, right engine! Warning! Warning! FTIT over temp, right engine!" I had an overheated right engine from a compressor stall that was critically near catching on fire.

All thoughts about the mission vanished. Now it was all about survival. I was a hundred miles off the coast of Savannah, at night, with thunderstorms all around me. Unless I got this situation under control, I'd have to punch out. Punching out of an F–15 is a harrowing, dangerous event, even in ideal conditions. My mind focused on the worst-case scenario: to eject a hundred miles off the coast, survive the water landing, wrestle with an inflatable one-man raft in a raging sea, fend off the sharks, and hope to be spot-

ted by rescue choppers at night was beyond dangerous. It was sui-
cidal.

But I wasn't actually doing anything to help myself, either,
because for some reason time seemed to stop; I froze. I know you'll
be able to sympathize. It happens to everyone. You're stressed out,
pressed for time, and all of a sudden something happens that
requires fast thinking and fast action. That's when that stress-
induced paralysis sets in. You freeze at the very moment that you
should be taking action. Any psychologist will tell you this is a
common reaction—our concentration is worst when our stress levels are the highest. The human brain is fallible, even in ideal conditions. In stressful conditions, it can be an absolute traitor.

So for a few precious seconds, surrounded by a sea flashing red
and yellow lights, I was completely brain-locked. I just couldn't
think. Then it came to me. *Pull out the checklist.* This is what a
checklist is for. Engine over-temps were common enough. The Air
Force had them in mind when they developed the emergency procedures checklist. *Pull out the checklist.* My hand reached down to
my G-suit pocket. I yanked the tab for "Emergency Procedures"
and there it was. Five immediate-action steps to take care of an
FTIT over-temp in flight. My mind and body sprang into action.
Hit this, do this, do that—whoosh—my engine relit. The red and
yellow lights quietly faded away. The thunderstorms suddenly didn't
seem so bad.

Shaken, tired, nervously happy to be alive, I flew the jet back to
Savannah, landed, went to the O-Club, and spent the rest of the
evening as a hero in my own mind. Everything was right with the
world. Task saturation lost again.

THREE WAYS TO OVERCOME TASK SATURATION

Everyone has emergencies. Modern life and modern business are
tough—tasks keep landing on your desk before the ones that are
already there are finished. Plans get washed away, the days get
short and tempers do, too. The problems come at you from all

sides and stack up until there seems to be no way out. Task saturation is knocking at your door.

But ask yourself—is it ever so tough that it approaches the danger level of a fighter pilot? In the everyday conduct of your business, can you make a mistake that can kill you? In our world, the answer is yes. Mistakes in our environment can be lethal. Which is why we spend enormous time and energy developing tools to overcome task saturation before it kills us. Perhaps not surprisingly, the tools are quite simple. In the chaos of that moment when you are utterly task-saturated, you want simple answers, simple actions, simple things to do to save you and your mission.

The Air Force places a high priority on helping pilots survive by enhancing their instant problem-solving capabilities. They have developed three ways of overcoming the negative effects of the silent killer—task saturation. The first is a physical object (the *checklist*); the second is a biomechanical process (*cross-checking*); and the third is a group dynamic (*mutual support*). They've all saved lives in flying situations—and they can all help save you in situations that might feel just as bad.

Checklists

My first day of F–15 flight school was about as disappointing as it gets. Did they introduce me to the jet I was about to fly? Did I climb up the ladder, have my picture taken, then get in and go for a familiarization flight? No, they handed me a four-inch-thick book and said, "Lieutenant, this is your DASH 1—your flight manual for the F–15. You need to know this book like the back of your hand. Learn it."

Now, the DASH–1 is no Tom Clancy novel. It's tough reading, thick with formulas and equations, and dense with text that reads like a foreign language. But it is The Book. It explains everything there is to know about the F–15. It outlines the performance characteristics, takeoff and landing gross weights, graphs, charts, operating procedures, exactly how the electrical system and the flight control systems work. It goes into intricate detail. It *is* the F–15, naked, its every tiny part broken down and explained.

I looked down at it and I had just one thought: *I'll never get through this.*

But what choice did I have?

Six months went by. I was totally involved, *immersed* in the flow of information. I studied and was tested, then studied and was tested again. And after six months I'd done it. I knew the book front-to-back. I could recall every page of every instruction on every procedure, sequence, and protocol. On paper, I knew the airplane inside and out.

But could I really retain this information on a long-term basis? Probably not. And where do you keep a four-inch-thick manual? It won't fit in the jet—and even if it did, the last thing you'd want to have to do in the heat of battle would be to page through it trying to find the heading for what you needed. That's why the Air Force uses checklists. Checklists are the distillation of that thick DASH–1 manual, keyworded and prioritized to communicate critical action steps quickly. They boil down the building blocks of training, and package them for speed and ease of use. Some checklists cover the basics, others are for emergencies. Either way, they have three things in common. They have been tested endlessly in simulators and in actual flight; they have been proven to work *without fail*; and they are easy to comprehend. Anything less would be a recipe for disaster.

Normal Procedures   The first section of the checklist is the normal procedures checklist. This list covers the actions a pilot repeats every time he goes aloft—preflight, starting, taxi, takeoff and landing, and other basic routines. These are all normally performed under very little time pressure, so the corresponding checklists can be longer and more detailed than an emergency procedures checklist.

Why use normal procedures checklists? Precisely because they *are* normal procedures. Normal procedures are *repeated* acts, and it's very easy to forget something you do so often that sometimes you can't remember that you did it. When I was a student pilot, it took me fifteen minutes to get all the switches into the right positions just to start the aircraft. Once I was proficient and had done it a hundred times, I was able to do it automatically. But automatic actions can be dangerous—you can convince yourself you've done something when maybe you haven't. That's where the normal procedures checklist comes in. By going down the list methodically, you make sure the everyday, routine acts have all been accomplished, that nothing has been taken for granted.

Not surprisingly, a great many businesses already use checklists, and for good reason. Our client Marriott uses them to make certain that every room has been completely cleaned and properly prepped for the next guest, that every item on the breakfast buffet is in place, and that all the reservation procedures are completed during the initial telephone call. The checklist helps Marriott minimize the number of errors made during routine procedures; it helps each employee double-check his own work and ensures high standards of uniform quality throughout the system.

Distribution centers are heavy users of normal procedures checklists. Think about the last time you ordered something from one of the hundreds—*thousands*—of mail order catalogs you've received. Now think about that order. One of this, one of that, a pair of these in blue, a dozen of those in white. To make sure you get that order, a picker goes into a warehouse and packs your box. In one hand he holds the items you've requested—and in the other, a checklist of your complete order. When your order arrived, did you notice anything else in the box? The return address labels, the packing slip, the special offers, the customer satisfaction survey? Guess how the picker remembered to include everything? Checklists.

Emergency Checklists   Emergency procedures checklists are quite different from normal procedures checklists. For one thing, they're *short*. They don't try to suggest long, labored solutions to fast-breaking problems. Emergency checklists cut to the chase—to the absolutely fundamental, critical steps necessary to solve a problem surely and quickly. The specific combination of emergency steps will have been thoroughly tested and proven to work flawlessly—no matter how bad your brain lock may be.

Interestingly, we actually have two levels of emergency checklists. Some emergencies require faster reaction than others. For instance, if I'm punching off my wing tanks and one of them hangs, it's an emergency but not necessarily a life-threatening one. I have a checklist for that, but it's a little more methodical, because timing isn't critical, and a little more detailed, because the solution isn't so simple.

But if I have an engine fire, I have just a few seconds before my F–15 might blow up in the sky. That checklist is *very* short. That checklist is called a *boldface*, because the steps we need to take to handle such an emergency are actually printed out in boldface on the card. Remember, things are chaotic enough in a bouncing, turning Mach 1 fighter like the F–15. Throw in a few dozen blinking lights and Bitchin' Betty in my ears, and the writing better be big.

Boldface steps are those items that are critical to aircraft recovery, control, or life-threatening emergencies. For every situation, there are just a few options to try. If any of them works, you'll recover. If not, the last item is usually the same—*Eject*. These are the pages that save your life.

Living with Checklists   The checklist concept sounds simple, but it isn't. It isn't enough to just write down the twenty items you need to do to open a McDonald's in the morning. The checklist must be tested with different types of employees and in different environments; then the entire staff needs to be trained in its use, so everyone understands the sequence of steps and knows how to use all the proper devices or tools.

But there's more. Checklists require maintenance. At Conco Paint, we had over fifty paint samples that were part of our standard presentation to home-center paint buyers. I discovered, though, that my guys were often trying to get by with only twenty or twenty-five of them; the others were forgotten in the backseats of their cars. To fix that, I made a checklist of everything that was supposed to be included in any sales presentation. I devised a "hit-and-run kit," which included everything a salesperson should carry into the store. I gave the kits to the entire sales force, and trained them in their proper use. My vice president loved this; he used to call the process *having your holster full* before going into the store.

It was a good idea and well received, but within weeks I learned something about checklists: If you want them to work *you've got to use them*—and use them completely. My sales force, I discovered, wasn't running the entire checklist before their presentations. I learned this when I went on sales calls with them; we'd walk in, and five minutes into the presentation my salesman would reach into his kit to show the buyer a sample—and come up empty-handed. Walking back to the car, I would turn to the rep and ask if he had used the checklist.

"Yes, I did."

"Did you really check the checklist before you left the car?"

"Not entirely."

"Okay, then, before you get out of your car at the next stop, I want you to go through the entire checklist and the entire kit, and make sure you have every single thing you need before you walk in." We got to the next sales call, the guy ran the checklist, and this time he had everything going into the meeting.

In the midst of a very hectic sales-call day, it can be easy to forget the small details. Task saturation does that. It doesn't matter how smart, how motivated or well-intentioned you are—you can still succumb to task saturation. A good checklist is a great way to save yourself from saturation-related errors.

After we instituted checklists at Conco, our sales performance improved tremendously. In fact, we found that paint buyers nationally were talking about the level of organization of our salesmen; sometimes they even read the contents of our hit-and-run kit aloud to their own employees. We got a reputation for being a well-prepared, squared-away bunch of guys, and the paint buyers always made time for us.

Standardizing Training   One place a checklist really works is in training. In the old days, new employees "shadowed" someone in their department and picked up what they needed to know by observation. There were no uniform practices in training, no procedural standards, and no standard expectations. New employees often learned little more than the good or bad habits of their trainer. In most industries, that doesn't happen anymore; today businesses are more efficient. Time is more precious, and training is more methodical.

Checklists are central to effective training. Think of all the time and energy that can be saved when an employee is handed a normal daily procedures checklist. On his first day he is taken through the entire department and shown how to do everything on it; thereafter, he should know every part of his job, and have a handy way to remind himself of its elements if he forgets. Then imagine having a checklist devoted to emergency procedures. If something out of the ordinary should happen during the workday—a can of paint falling from a high perch and splattering all over the floor; the computer going down; an irate customer creating a scene—the emergency procedures list swings into action. Right there in black and white are simple, step-by-step instructions for dealing with virtually all contingencies. The emergency procedures checklist anticipates the event and shows *proper, proven, time-tested* procedures for dealing with it. An employee, even the newest, rawest kid in the plant, can quickly refer to the checklist and start fixing the problem.

Some employers have expressed the concern that such checklists might seem demeaning to their employees, but in my experience and that of companies who've reported their success to us, the exact opposite is true. In fact, checklists can be liberating in their comprehensiveness, and employees can derive great peace of mind from their use: When you see that your particular problem is covered in the checklist, you know someone has already faced the problem before—and has already found the right thing to do. There's nothing more empowering than giving employees a way to solve their problems quickly, dependably, and on the ground floor, without having to appeal to management.

Checklists, though, aren't meant to compensate for employees who can't think for themselves. Personality and intuition are often the secrets to a good transaction with a customer, and in training your crew to use checklists it's important to make sure they understand that they should supplement the list's recommendations with their own common sense. Nothing is a bigger turnoff than an employee with an inflexible, automated response.

Should your checklists be chiseled in stone? Yes and no. Some situations do call for absolutes—many finite problems have established solutions. But things change. Checklists have to be dynamic. We in the fighter pilot community update our checklists *weekly*. Equipment improvements, upgraded performance characteristics, new radio frequencies, and physical changes to air bases around the world all make it imperative that pilot checklists be up-to-date. Be ready to update your checklists. That is a part of management's job—to keep its eye on innovations and changes in the environment, and work the changes into a newer, better, more current checklist. Many of the changes come from the people *using* checklists, so keep an ear open when you talk to your people, too. The best ideas are sometimes right under your nose.

Cross-Checks

If you're a pilot, your primary job is to maintain control of your aircraft. Your secondary job will vary with each mission, but no matter what type of jet you're flying, your primary job is maintaining aircraft control. In other words, *Don't hit the ground, or anything attached to it.* The secret to maintaining aircraft control is in the effective use of what we call *attitude checks*. By attitude checks, we don't mean coming to work with a smile on your face. What we're talking about is checking the physical position of the aircraft relative to the horizon, as tracked by an instrument called the *attitude indicator*. The most important instrument in any aircraft cockpit, the attitude indicator is located dead center in the middle of the instrument panel, and it's the biggest instrument we have. What does it look like? The face of the instrument contains a graphic reproduction of the earth—the bottom of it is black or brown, like the ground, and the top is blue or white, like the sky. If you're flying along and you see more black than you do white, you're descending. If you see more white than black, you're ascending. If the ball is tilted right or left, it indicates that the aircraft is in a bank. Can you see why that's so important?

But there are other instruments in the cockpit that are absolutely critical, too—the altimeter, the heading indicator, the fuel gauge, the air speed indicator, the radar. They all need to be monitored, as surely as the attitude indicator. So the problem arises: How can anyone monitor all these gauges at the same time? This cockpit dilemma is a special version of task saturation, and one that will be familiar to anyone in the business world—*How can I handle all these tasks at once?* One answer is by instituting a habit of cross-checks.

Pilots have developed a biomechanical process that allows them to maintain near-simultaneous monitoring of multiple instruments—a practice called *cross-checking*. Cross-checking involves an active scan of all the instruments on the instrument panel. The instrument cross-check always starts with the attitude indicator and the question *Are the wings level?* If they aren't, the pilot makes a quick adjustment, then quickly checks the other instruments. The pilot shifts his focus to the altimeter *for a second*, then recenters his sight back on the attitude indicator. Are they level yet? No, but they're on their way. Boom, back to the other instruments—maybe the heading indicator, making sure he is still flying the heading he was assigned—*but then shifts his gaze right back to the attitude indicator*. There, wings level. He does this with every switch and dial in the cockpit, always coming back to the center within seconds, to the attitude indicator. He never stops asking, *Am I maintaining aircraft control? Are my wings straight and level?*

As we saw in the Eastern 401 example, channelizing on a single instrument can be deadly. On the other hand, admittedly, it can be tempting to *watch* the heading indicator as you change headings. But a good pilot knows he can't fall into that trap. He can only look for a second, then come back to the attitude indicator, then back to the heading indicator, then back again. When a pilot gets channelized, or focuses on one of the peripheral instruments too long, the plane can easily get out of control.

Business Attitude Checks   Any successful company watches the core of its business as if it were an attitude indicator: *Are core sales going up? How about market share? Are we competitive enough?* But business is always changing, and nowadays there are global factors tugging it in a hundred different directions. There's the constant and understandable temptation to focus resources on problem areas, or on one department, or on one tantalizing opportunity. But if you don't come back and check your attitude—the fundamentals of your business—every few seconds, you'll end up flying off in some unexpected direction or, worse, flying right into the ground.

Microsoft, for all its success, nearly crashed and burned at one point in its history. Microsoft knows its core business is operating systems. DOS and Windows, the brand names of its main operating systems, have an incredible share of market. Microsoft can and does do everything to keep DOS/Windows the dominant PC operating systems on the market.

But some years ago Microsoft channelized. It focused on the DOS/Windows share-of-market instrument to the exclusion of its attitude indicator. While it was channelizing on share-of-market, the customers were swinging away from the company and running toward something called the Internet. Operating systems weren't such a big deal anymore; the talk had shifted. The business world was focusing its attention on the possibilities of the Internet, but Microsoft wasn't. Microsoft was so channelized on OS's that it almost missed one of the most fundamental shifts in the digital age.

But not for long. Bill Gates *was* sweeping the instruments, checking the attitude indicator, and guess what—he noticed the ten-degree bank to the right. He saw that his company had fallen out of step with the market. So he rushed resources into play. Yes, Netscape and America Online used the momentary gap when Microsoft was channelized to carve out their niches. But Microsoft soon had Explorer and the Microsoft Network in the game. Its cross-checks kept Microsoft in step with its customers—a life-saving necessity for all companies.

3Com Corporation had a similar dilemma—in its case because it had an unexpected *success* on its hands. 3Com has a product called the Palm Computer. At the end of 1999, it was by far the leading "personal digital assistant"—and sales were galloping up the charts like a Thor missile coming off the launchpad. But 3Com's board was troubled. Its read of the attitude indicator said that the company was too focused on the Palm and not spending enough time on its core business, which was networking gear for computers. Despite the incredible success of its new product, the board unanimously voted to spin off the little widget with $500 million in sales and concentrate on its $5.2 *billion* core business.

Mutual Support

Remember the expression "Never leave your wingman"? The movie *Top Gun* brought that phrase into mainstream usage. But what does it mean? To a fighter pilot it means building *mutual support roles* in the everyday execution of our missions. You may notice that jets are virtually always flown in multiples of twos. There is a very sound tactical reason for this. Like lone animals in Africa who stray from the herd, lone aircraft in enemy territory get picked off.

A two-ship formation of aircraft is the fighter pilot's fundamental offensive and defensive building block. Simple math tells you that a two-ship doubles the guns and missiles available to employ against a threat. Double a two-ship to a four-ship, and you double again the offensive and defensive firepower. Two-ships double the "eyes" out of the cockpit, double the radar scan of the airspace, double the what-if-ing, and double the level of confidence we have in the sky.

Here's an example of mutual support in action. In air combat, a pilot's most vulnerable position is to his rear (his six, or six o'clock position). Heat-seeking missiles aim at your engine nozzles, which are at your six, and you can't see out the back without turning around. But you *have* to know what's going on back there. Therefore, pilots are always checking six—that is, looking over their shoulders for enemy missiles and enemy aircraft.

In a two-ship formation, checking six works as mutual support for both pilots. In fact, it's part of the motherhood procedures. After a pilot checks his own six, his next responsibility is the six of his wingman—and his wingman's responsibility is the lead's six. Back and forth it goes, each pilot sweeping the airspace behind the other, mutually supporting each other in the game to check six.

Sadly, the exact opposite of mutual support is often more visible in today's workplace. All the many varieties of internal competition—rivalries, secrecy, job retention worries, personal ambitions, and other human frailties—are vital threats to successful teamwork, often derailing management's attempts to unite its workforce into a supportive group. No protocol can eliminate all interpersonal problems, but a corporate culture that encourages mutual support roles stands to win in the long run. Let me give you three examples.

Backups   Nothing works *against* mutual support more than a my-kingdom mentality, in which everyone does his own job and protects his own desk and his own turf, and doesn't worry about the person five feet away. But what happens when a key employee is ill or incapacitated? Who knows what projects he was working on, what stage those projects were in, what the budgets were, what the deadlines are? Who's going to pick up where the other left off? A company whose employees have been trained in mutual support will be more likely to avoid such disasters, by emulating that old Broadway mindset we discussed earlier and having an understudy in place so that the show can go on.

Inter-Employee Cross-Checks   Task saturation is everywhere in American business, at all levels in all companies. The employees who are affected most dramatically often can't see that they are channelizing on low-priority items or flying off-course; remember, task saturation is the *silent* killer. But if there's a coworker nearby who knows the flight plan—a wingman, so to speak—he should be able to recognize the problem and bring the team back on track. In marketing departments, some companies divide people along product lines. The brand manager for one item sits next to the brand manager for another item, but they often haven't the slightest idea what the other is doing. Introducing mutually supportive roles would help the brand managers help each other. Countless studies have proven the benefits of cross-checking, self-correcting project *teams* in action.

Stress Reduction   Knowing that you don't have to carry a heavy burden alone can be a great stress reliever for most business people. We all try to work hard, and we don't like asking for help, but wouldn't it be a tremendous relief to know that in your company there were others who are up to speed on your projects, and who could be called on to step in and help with the workload if need be? Introducing a network of mutual employee support can be a logical way to ensure that the normal daily work flow of your company isn't hampered by overreliance on any one person who may be suffering under the weight of too much responsibility, but is nevertheless unwilling or unable to admit the problem.

SUMMARY

1. Every company should incorporate an employee training program that includes a policy and work rules manual—a booklet featuring a series of written checklists of everyday and emergency procedures. This will help every employee to know and understand his daily duties in priority order, and to react properly (and alone if need be) in any unusual or emergency situation that crops up during the business day. The use of checklists is an empowering technique that localizes problems, speeds up solutions, and ultimately provides exceptional customer service.

2. Another powerful productivity tool is the use of cross-checks, which is simply a mental discipline that returns one's focus to the core of one's business, rather than dwelling on the fringes. Managers should be especially attuned to the need to keep abreast of their business's basic mission and attitude, even in the face of the constant distractions of the everyday business environment.

3. Mutual support systems can help create a dynamic work environment in which employees work as a team, guarding each others' flanks, keeping the target in sight, helping out wherever help is needed, and keeping everything running smoothly no matter how many "casualties" there are.

Taken together, all three of these tools offer the perfect antidote to the insidious threat of task saturation, the disease that can cause pilots and companies alike to die relaxed.

THE DEBRIEF: THE LAND OF NO SLACK

I was flying back from a seminar in Boston when four people rushed on my flight and tumbled into the seats across the aisle from me. After they buckled in, the conversation started to roll. It was obvious from the bits and pieces that I picked up that they'd just finished a major sales presentation. The snippets were interesting: "Man, we had 'em, didn't we!" And then I heard, "Did you see the look on Eddie's face when they asked about the deliveries? Eddie, you sure know how to dance." And finally I heard, "Hey, we were close, we did good. Chalk it up to experience."

Now, don't get me wrong, I like to have fun as much as the next guy—but what do you suppose these people got out of their impromptu, post–sales call meeting? Nothing. Sure, they blew off a little steam and that's all right, but let me make a suggestion: Don't let the sales day be over until you debrief. Wait till later to blow off steam. *Debrief* your meeting first.

THE DEBRIEF

When we touch down after every air combat mission, we're happy to be home safely, but we know it isn't Miller time yet. Not by a long shot. I've told you that as soon as the canopy pops open the intel people coming running out with their question sheet. Well, after that, we've got about ten minutes to climb out of the jet, walk to the squadron shack, stow our equipment, hit the head, wash up, and take care of any squawks—mechanical trouble—the jet may have. After that, we're all due back in the briefing room for the debrief.

Follow me through this, because debriefing is one of the most important strategies you can introduce to your company. I absolutely, positively guarantee that efficiency will rise dramatically for you, for your people, and for your company, if you learn to debrief properly.

Top Gun

Despite the fact that our adversaries were often flying older, slower MiG–15s and MiG–17s during the Vietnam War the United States Air Force had a terrible air-to-air kill ratio against the North Vietnamese. We were flying a great jet, the F–4 Phantom, and we had tons of technology. But we couldn't do much better than a two-to-one kill ratio, which is totally unacceptable for us. Something had to be done about that, and a joint Air Force/Navy study was commissioned. What they learned was a revelation: If a pilot survived his first few missions in Vietnam, his survival and efficiency rating went through the roof. In short, they learned just how true the old saw is: Experience counts. All we needed was to create a pilot training center that could *accelerate experience*. Out of that came what are now called the Navy's Top Gun School and the Air Force's Fighter Weapons School. But what most people don't know is that something else came out of that study—*a process*. In addition to learning how to fly against dissimilar aircraft, which is at the heart of Top Gun, *we began to learn how to brief, execute, and debrief air combat missions*.

You've already seen the fruits of what we learned about briefing and executing. We learned even more about *de*briefing. The Air Force/Navy study revealed that our debriefs hadn't been debriefs at all. Pilots would land from a mission, get out of their jets, talk on the ramp, toss a few ideas around, and that was that. When we did have a formal debrief, it would amount to no more than a rehash of what had happened in the air. There was no true structure, and we were failing to do the most important thing—systematically identifying our mistakes as a way of improving on our future performance. With the advent of Top Gun, all that changed. The character and intensity of the debriefs went up several magnitudes; later, as the Top Gun pilots filtered back out to their units, they spread the new debriefing gospel to other pilots.

Today, the debrief is one of the cornerstone doctrines of the fighter community. And it's the kind of simple but revolutionary process that could stand to remake much of American business.

What Is a Debrief?

The debrief is the bookend to the preflight mission brief, and it's just as serious as its mate. It is not about demeaning or browbeating people. Its purpose is to deconstruct, analyze, talk about, and view (by means of videotape or electronic range information) the mission that just transpired, and to identify the mistakes that were made along the way. Because of this, we *always* have a debrief after *every* mission. Every pilot who took part in the mission is in attendance—*and attendance is mandatory*.

You'll recall that ideally our mission objective, as stated in the preflight brief, was clear, measurable, and achievable. The motherhood and mission tactics were well laid out. The contingencies were put on the table. The pilots seemed satisfied, with no questions left unanswered. *On paper*, such a mission should go flawlessly—but it doesn't always work that way. Missions rarely go off without hitches.

The debrief is the place where everybody's hitches are hauled out in front of everybody else, where we find out why the mistakes happened and what's going to be done to prevent the same mistakes from occurring in the future. Let me repeat—we throw our mistakes right out in the open, talk about them, discuss ways to prevent them from happening again, then get on with it. The debrief is about ongoing improvement. The only way to do that is to shine a light on the screw-ups, and make each pilot accountable for his actions. Letting things slide and looking the other way is not the Air Force way. There's too much at stake. If we make mistakes the mission objective may not be reached, the bombs may not get to the target, and people may die. That's why they call the debrief *the land of no slack*. Are we professional in the debriefing room? Yes. But are we society-polite? No.

Some Ground Rules

Any company looking to set up a system of debriefings for its mission teams must first be aware of a few ground rules. In fact, you can't have effective debriefs if you don't follow these rules. They may seem at odds with the great struggle to climb the corporate ladder, but you can't tap the magic of a fighter pilot debrief without them.

1. Rankless—Nameless

The most important of our ground rules—the one that allows people to say what they need to say—is this: *There is no rank and no naming of names in the debriefing room*. There may have been a one-star general, a captain, a colonel, and several lieutenants in a particular flight, but when you walk into a debrief, everyone leaves rank at the door. For the duration, everybody is the same—there is no seniority; there are no presidents or vice presidents. The only person with authority in the room is the flight lead. He briefed the mission. He debriefs the mission. And he can be criticized, too. In a military debriefing, it's also strict policy that *no names* are used; the whole idea of a debrief is to undertake a strict analysis of the execution of a mission, and getting personal tends to create barriers that can make it harder to learn from one's mistakes. In the Air Force, our names and ranks are printed on Velcro name tags; this is done for a lot of reasons—one is to make it harder for the enemy to identify us if we get shot down—but it's also the case that some squadrons have you rip off your name tag and throw it in a bucket as you come into the debriefing, to emphasize the importance of anonymity in the debriefing room.

It may seem less practical in a business environment, but you should try to find ways to get rid of names in your debriefing sessions as well. The spirit of debriefing is to emphasize the group and its improvement. By their very nature, names are about individuals. If the flight lead says, "Murph, why didn't you lock at twenty-five miles?" he's pointing me out personally, which may raise my hackles and add a distracting emotional edge to the proceedings. Instead of doing that, we call each other by our tactical call signs. It feels less personal, and that minimizes defensive behavior.

2. No Fear of Reprimand

The second ground rule is this: *Admit your mistakes right up front; there is no fear of reprimand in the debrief.* Each pilot has a responsibility to highlight his own screw-ups. At the very least, admitting you made a mistake shows that you were mentally alert enough during the mission to recognize what you did wrong. *Not* knowing you made a mistake is in many ways worse. But, either way, the second element of this rule is paramount: Even though a general or a colonel may be sitting next to you, no reprimands or any personal criticisms resulting from mistakes made in the mission are allowed within the confines of the debrief. This is the only way to ensure that everyone speaks fully and freely, without fear of repercussions.

I recall a situation when four of us were flying an exercise—a colonel, a captain (me), and two lieutenants. I was the flight lead. In my briefing I had said that we were going to lock our radars at twenty-five miles, and we would have missiles in the air by twenty miles. But in the debrief, when we looked at our gun camera tapes and our radar tapes, we realized that everybody was locked at twenty-five miles except the colonel—and that everybody had had missiles in the air at twenty miles except the colonel. We lost two Eagles on that day's mission, and you could see on the tapes that we lost them because of the colonel. Well, I can tell you, the colonel, who felt terrible, was the first person to admit his mistakes. First of all, he knew the tapes were going to be played, so we would all be seeing his mistakes anyway. But he knew that the debriefing room wasn't the place to be a colonel, that his ego had no place here at all. So he admitted the mistakes right away. He's a fighter pilot. I'm a fighter pilot. On this mission he fell short—and he acknowledged his error, making it far easier for us all to learn from what happened.

Now, we could have taken the colonel's mistakes and swept them under the carpet. No point in antagonizing the brass, right? Wrong! Not only would that have been a disservice to the colonel, who might have flown again the next day without learning from his mistakes, and risk dire consequences; it would also have left the two new lieutenants, who had limited flight experience, unaware of the colonel's mistakes. Instead, everyone benefited from understanding exactly what happened—and from seeing that it could happen to anyone. Admitting one's mistakes is a surefire way to create a cohesive group; the ability to talk openly creates an indisputable feeling of camaraderie, bonding the group together and engendering pride in one's job.

3. *Mission Participants Only*

Remember this one last rule and never break it: *The debrief is a gathering of the mission participants only.* No sit-ins by others who were not involved should be allowed under any circumstances. Even if it's your CEO who wants to attend a debrief, find a way to avoid it. The very intimate nature of a debrief would be destroyed by the presence of a party who wasn't there—an onlooker with no previous investment in the mission, who would only make the others feel judged and uncomfortable. Never allow it to happen.

THE ELEMENTS OF A DEBRIEF

In our fighter pilot debriefs we have one advantage that you won't: We videotape our missions. All of our F–15s have two videotape recorders on board; one tapes the radar display and records all the communications both inside and outside the jet, while the other looks through the heads up display (HUD) and records what we saw facing forward.

When we debrief, we all bring in our tapes; they are cued and time-synched so that they're ready to be reviewed at the appropriate time. Then we sit down and turn our attention to the lead.

Here's what follows:

1. *Reiterate the Objective*

The debrief is structured much like the preflight briefing. The first thing we do is to reiterate the mission objective. The flight lead will start the debrief by asking, "Did everybody understand the mission objective?" Now, why would he ask that? We stated the mission objective hours ago in the briefing. We just flew the mission itself. Indeed, before we left for the mission, nobody had any questions about the objective. Well, there are three reasons: to give the debrief *crystal-clear focus,* to align all of the subsequent comments with the original objective, and to make sure people really understood it as they flew. If somebody says, "Yeah, I was unclear on your targeting plan when I walked out the door," then there's a problem, and you deal with this basic type of problem first.

So what do you do when someone says he was unclear about the objective? There are really only two possible reasons someone would say such a thing. Perhaps the pilot is a numskull who forgot to ask the question initially. If that's true, the leader has to make the point that no one should ever leave the original brief with an unanswered question. The other possibility is that the flight lead's mission objective wasn't communicated as clearly as it should have been. If that's the case, lead should make a mental note to stress the mission objective next time, and make absolutely certain everyone understands it.

2. *Start with Self-Criticism*

Once you've restated the mission objective and determined whether it was clear, you jump directly into the meat of the meeting. To do that, you have to prime the pump, and here's where a little humility helps. The first thing the lead has to do is open up communication, and one way to do that is to admit his own mistakes first. If it were my debrief I might say something like this: "Everybody knows basically what the outcome of the mission was, but right off the bat I want to apologize because this morning's preflight briefing started a few minutes late and I know that kind of rushed us. You guys didn't have time to hit the head, get all your equipment on, which in turn rushed our start procedures. Number two, I know you were late checking in, which kind of typified the entire mission today. We were one step behind today all the way up and down, and I take full responsibility for that since I started the briefing late. Another thing I know that I didn't do right is when I got out to the arming area, I had briefed everybody that we were going to take off at twenty-second radar trail, and when we went out to the runway I gave you an audible takeoff at ten seconds. I'm sorry I did that, and I know it was another big change to my briefing. I'll get into some of the tactical things that I know I did wrong later, but those are some of the big things that I did wrong early." Boom! What has that done? It has just put me on level ground with everybody else. They're looking at me, thinking, *That's pretty cool. This guy hasn't pointed his finger at any of us for screwing up; instead he's taking some responsibility himself, right from the start.*

In the very next breath, I'll ask, "Before we get started: Number Two"—again, I'm not using his name—"is there anything you think I could have done better in my briefing? Or is there anything that you saw me do out there, motherhood-wise, that could have made this mission go more smoothly?"

Now, this guy will inevitably be thinking, *Great, here's my boss asking me to throw a spear at him—what does he think I am, crazy?* I know from years of experience that the first comment will be mild; Number Two might say, "Well, Murph, because of the weather and a late scheduling change, you got a little bit rushed. Under the circumstances, though, I thought you did a great job today."

A pointless comment, isn't it? You have to get right through that person right away, because the first guy's comments are almost never useful. But make that person feel good by saying, "I appreciate that, but I know that I made some mistakes. Number Three, what do you have for me?" He says, "Lead, you put the formation looking into the sun. I had a hard time seeing the bogeys in the glare." Now we're getting somewhere. This is the type of incisive comment I'm looking for. I'll reward Three by agreeing with him and piggybacking on his statement. Press on with your questioning, and you'll find the comments will get sharper with each subsequent person *until you really start talking about the mission.* Once the real daggers have flown, then don't ask for any more. You've made your point. You're just trying to establish open communication and, if there are valid criticisms, improve your personal execution.

3. *Revisit the Plan As Originally Briefed*

So far we've only restated the mission objective and critiqued my role in the motherhood portion of the mission. The next thing you want to do is revisit the plan, which means revisiting the brief. All the people in the room have just executed a plan that you developed, and either you got stomped, or you were extremely successful, or somewhere in between. Win or lose, everybody now has a common experience, and each one of them should now be able to make some valid comment on how well your plan worked. At this point I might say, "This is what we decided we were going to do today. We were going to start off at 30,000 feet; we were going to do this, this, and this." I'll give them a very quick update of the original briefing. Then I'd ask, "Is that the way you all remember it?"

Notice that I keep coming back to this question—"Is that the way you all remember it?" This is a very effective way of breaking down the execution of your plan: Either you told them to fire missiles at twenty miles or you didn't, either they *did* fire at twenty miles or they didn't, but if they all remember the original plan being set up differently, then the problem wasn't in the execution but in the vagueness of the original brief. Conversely, if everyone remembers being briefed to fire at twenty miles, then when I turn to Two to talk about why he failed to fire at twenty we'll be well past the point of excuses or bickering over interpretation.

With luck, everybody will agree that he understood the plan. Again, if there are still outstanding questions, then you are going to have to question yourself on your briefing style, how well your briefing was laid out, how clear it was. Conversely, you might also have to question your subordinates' abilities to absorb or carry out the kind of plan you presented—maybe it was too complex for them. The important thing is that you asked, and you've learned something from their responses.

4. *Analyze the Execution: Who, Where, When, and Why*

Our next step is to analyze the execution, and that means it's showtime. This is when we roll the tapes and see who got shot, who got their missiles off the rails, and all the other details of the mission, burned on videotape for everyone to see in stark black and white. If four jets flew the mission, four tapes will play at the same time; we get to see everything, hear everything, watch ourselves make our mistakes. We look at communications errors, shot errors, formation errors, execution errors, and tactical errors. Then we identify each type of error, who made it, when it was made, where he made it, and why.

With that level of detail, it is a rare debrief that releases anybody unscathed.

A useful way to analyze a mission is to start with the gross mistakes that you, as the leader, couldn't see during the mission. For example, on the tapes I'll notice a mistake, and I'll say, "Number Three, what were you thinking there? I notice you didn't lock until eighteen miles; can you tell me what your thought process was?" He probably just forgot, so I get a good chance to point this out and give us all a lesson learned. But maybe he'll say something like, "Well, you briefed that if we didn't lock by twenty-five miles, you wanted us to fall back into this formation. But the sun was low on the horizon at three o'clock and you had me on the left side of the formation, looking into the sun. So it took me extra time to adjust my spacing, which made me late with my lock. I also knew that that would highlight the formation if I did it the way it was briefed." Well, that's a revelation for me, and in my next briefing I'll know to address that contingency up front. One lesson learned by me.

Next, debrief the fine points. It's in the fine points that the real problems sometimes dwell, the ones that could kill you on the next mission. For example, we'll listen to our radio communication, because in the briefing we'll already have discussed how we were going to talk on the radios for this particular engagement. Then we'll debrief our radars. The F–15 has complex radar software, and it's a taxing piece of equipment to work, but if someone makes a mistake—failing to monitor the level of airspace he was assigned, for example—I will dwell on the mistake to the point of pain. I will really drive home the importance of complete radar coverage. And if he squirms, that's all right. He'll know he screwed up, but he won't be angry; he'll more likely be eager to fly with me again, to show me he can do it right . . . and also to watch for my mistakes. He'll be only too happy to point out every little thing I did wrong at the next debrief. And that's okay, too.

5. *Recap the Mission Outcome*

After all the errors have been analyzed, the leader needs to recap the mission, again using rhetorical questions: "The mission objective was to eliminate airborne threats in our lane of responsibility, to have outstanding communications, 100 percent valid weapons, no aborts, and zero people die. How did we do? Did we meet our mission objective? First, did we provide air superiority for the thirty-two-minute vulnerability time? Based on the radar tapes, no. Number Two did not cover the surface-to-10,000-foot block on the left side, and a bandit sneaked into our lane. Next, did we have outstanding communication, no communications errors? No, we didn't. We just heard that Number Two and Number Four made minor communications deviations. We've identified those mistakes and why they were made. Next, did we have 100 percent valid shots? Yes, based on the tapes, everybody here employed 100 percent valid shots. Good job. Next, did we have zero aborts? No, Number Three had to abort on our second pump because of a radar system failure. Number Three is going to huddle with the radar techs as soon as we leave here to sort out that problem. Last, did anybody get killed? No, everybody made it, so good job there."

6. *Lessons Learned*

The whole point of the debrief is to improve. By highlighting our mistakes we help eliminate them in the future. Sometimes, however, we discover a mistake that the rest of the squadron should know about. I mentioned earlier that we treat crashes as important lessons learned. Well, smaller errors of execution also get chalked up as lessons learned, but when we come upon an executional mistake we post it for the entire squadron to see and read. We don't attach names to it; we just post a page with the heading "Lessons Learned on Mission One," and that way the guys on mission number two can get an early warning about potential problems. That kind of posting also gives the lead for mission two the chance to improve his brief: "Hey, the guys who did the mission this morning got burned here, so let's change the brief in the following ways." It's a great way to learn.

7. *End on the Positives*

A good debrief should always, always end on the positive aspects of the mission, no matter how ugly the mission was, no matter how many mistakes were made. There is always *something* positive about a mission; the best strategy is to leave the crew with at least a gesture of goodwill by pointing it out. Often it's worth reiterating that you understand these debriefs can feel negative, because they're all about pointing out mistakes, but that ultimately everyone will improve as a result. Highlight the best parts of what went on, underscore how difficult doing anything right was (if that's the case), but find the positives. Then thank the group, grab your name tag out of the bucket, press it back on your chest, and leave the room. Finally, it's Miller time.

THE DEBRIEF IN BUSINESS

If there's one opportunity that almost every company in America is missing, it's the benefits that come with undertaking regular post-mission debriefings. In fact, debrief *avoidance* is much more often the norm, built into corporate behavior from California to New York, Alaska to Texas. We fighter pilots have feelings, we are human, but we finish every mission we fly with a raw, in-the-gut debrief. Willingly. Openly. Why? Because it's a helluva lot better than dying.

If you do nothing else to change your way of doing business, do this one thing—set up a mandatory debriefing system. If a product rollout fails, or a new store opening goes flat, or a monthly sales quota is not met, it might seem like the easiest or most humane thing to do to forget about it and look ahead to next campaign. *Don't do it.* Hold a formal debrief. If a product is a success or a new procedure works flawlessly, do the same. Avoiding a debrief is like not opening the mail or hiding under your bedcovers when you hear a bump in the night. After all, if one salesperson doesn't meet quota, your whole bottom line can start to tilt off-center, and then you run the risk of losing control.

Most companies resist the debriefing idea at first, usually for what seem like considerate reasons. After all, no one really wants to point out that someone has missed quota; it can make everyone feel uncomfortable. Most managers would rather say, "Joe, I know you didn't make quota for us last month, but just try to make it next month. I know you can do it. What can you do next month? Can you hit 30,000 next month? Good, 30,000 is your quota for next month."

But why didn't Joe meet his quota *this* month? Maybe it was management's problem: Maybe the mission objective was too high. Okay, then management needs to reassess its products and market research. Maybe. But maybe Joe made some mistakes, too. Maybe Joe used the old missiles, or the old tactics you've been try-ing to eliminate for months. Maybe you *know* he used the old stuff. Do you really want to stand aside as the company misses its sales goals, as you miss your own bonuses, as your group starts to drift to the bottom of the pack? Do you really want to fail for the sake of protecting Joe's ego? I hope not. And, if you have new salespeople in the room, wouldn't an analysis of Joe's performance be a training opportunity, a standard-setting threshold?

Another common excuse for avoiding debriefings stems from an undeniable truth. Business moves too fast, managers complain.

Goals are changing all the time, and so are quotas, and products, and competition—even the salespeople themselves. It isn't long before this month's missed goals are last month's old news. But no business can afford to hide behind the skirts of an excuse like that for very long—not when inferior performance is slowly hurting the company. Last month, or last selling season, or last year, may be over, but the bug is still in the system. The reasons for under-performance are almost always hidden below the surface—until the next time a new product comes down to the sales department, when they'll just raise their ugly heads all over again.

Without debriefing, chronic problems are carried over from one mission to the next and the next, until finally someone looks up and starts wondering why nothing is working. That's the beauty of a fighter pilot mission debrief—while the mission elements are still fresh in everyone's mind, the group examines what went right, and what went wrong. And, yes, they identify who screwed up. But that's not a bad thing. In a properly held debrief, the mission's mistakes can be identified and discussed without personal animosity, blame, negative energy, anger, confrontation, or resentment. It sounds impossible, I know. But conducted responsibly, the debrief is the only sure way to weed out problems and focus the company's energy on the future.

Accountability

When my Afterburner Seminar participants hear the story of the colonel taking criticism from a captain, they always say, "That would never work here." Why wouldn't it work? They say, "Well, we have a pecking order here; our bosses are our bosses . . ." I just look at them and say, "You don't think we have a pecking order in the military? We wear a rank on our shoulders! A one-star general can have me shot!"

Generals are powerful people. When a general visits another base, word spreads in advance that a DV (distinguished visitor) is on the way. Lawns get mowed, hedges get trimmed, an actual red carpet comes out of the base office. When a one-star general comes into a room, you stand up, you snap to attention—*you salute him.* The whole *building* comes to attention, and nobody sits down until he says, "As you were." You even salute his *car.* That is how much power this guy carries on a military base.

But an Air Force general who flies in a mission is just like everybody else. In fact, he is usually a wingman and not a flight lead. If I tell the general not to shoot his missiles, he knows that's the way it's got to be. If I tell him to notch and leave—that is, to go ninety degrees to try to break a radar lock and then abort—he notches and leaves. He wouldn't radio me and say, "Why are you doing that, soldier?" There is absolutely no time for debate in air combat.

The reason for this is a crucial military principle, and it's another idea that's widely underemphasized in corporate America: accountability. When we fly a mission, everyone involved understands that for the duration of that mission he is accountable to the leader for the success of that mission—whether he's a new lieutenant or a general with thousands of hours of flying time. Ultimately, the weakest-link theory holds here: It doesn't matter if it's the lieutenant or the general who screws up his assignment—if someone blows it, we miss our objective. The same should be true in business. If a senior vice president screws up a presentation, it hurts your company—*your* company. Winning in the combat of business should be a greater priority than preserving the ego of your combatants. Great people show their greatness in their humility and their approachability and in their ability to put the goals of the organization above their egos.

Almost Doesn't Count

A growing number of companies have put in place some kind of debriefing policy; often it's called *360-degree feedback* or a *post-mortem* or an *after-action meeting.* But many such programs have weaknesses that make them ineffective. Let me point out a few, with some recommendations on how to begin the debrief process in your company.

1. Business Debriefs Are Often Too Infrequent to Be Effective

One of the reasons military debriefings work is that they're constant. We fighter pilots are accustomed to debrief; they're part of our work cycle, and we've long ago lost any feelings of intimidation they might have aroused.

Businesses, on the other hand, tend to hold debriefs infrequently and formally—which makes them feel more like an audit committee review than a group forum intended for everybody's gain. The first commitment you have to make when you commit to holding debriefs is to make them part of the work cycle. Only if they occur with everyday regularity are they likely to lead to the kind of free and open exchange from which everyone can benefit.

2. The Timing of Business Debriefs Is Usually Wrong

For us pilots, debriefs are crucial to the job. They don't come at the expense of our other duties; they *are* part of our duties. When we're in the debriefing room, we don't feel as if we're supposed to be somewhere else, or that we're holding back others from getting something done because we're in the debrief. If we did, the debrief would be undermined by tapping fingers, restless pilots, and people knocking on the door.

Businesses who have debriefs often try to shove them in between work activities, as if they somehow constitute a stolen hour or a coffee break. A paint department's team meetings, for example, might be squeezed in on a Monday morning, with management and team leaders agitating to get them over with so they can return to the work at hand. But, as we've seen, briefings and debriefings can't be made to seem haphazard or rushed if they're to be effective. Instead, they should be regularly scheduled events, during which everyone involved is exempt from any other commitments; attendance must be mandatory, and other employees should be expected to work around them.

3. Define Your Participants

The fighter pilot squadron is an easy unit to define, but most businesses harbor similarly organic groups. An advertising agency or an accounting firm or even a law firm may have a new-business team, for example—a team that pitches new accounts on behalf of the firm. These are the people who are proficient at explaining the company's heritage, current accounts, operating methods, and company structure. This is a good example of a well-defined team—and the kind of team that would likely debrief together.

There are departments in every retail operation, and there are crew shifts in almost every service business; each of these constitutes a definable business unit. I can't tell you how often I've heard CEOs tell me that they used the opportunity of implementing debriefs to reevaluate the entire structure of their organizations. The Air Force recognizes the unity and the power of the squadron as a basic unit of the military organization; you, too, should try to determine the basic unit of your organization. Is it a shift, a department, or a brand group? If your business involves important tasks such as new-business pitches that are repeated frequently and consistently, why not organize a new-business squadron that can handle them as a permanent team? With time—and with the useful tool of regular debriefs—a homogeneous working team can become a powerful group of rainmakers for your organization.

4. Debrief While You're Fresh

To make a debrief a "morning after" meeting is to miss the whole point. Debriefs are only effective while you're still fresh, even if everyone in the room is exhausted. The founder of a great air show in the Midwest has a mandatory debrief at the end of the day on each of the three days of the show. Tired, haggard, worn down by the tens of thousands of people that come and go with questions and complaints, he still insists that the entire show management team attend the debriefs just as soon as the gates close. Everyone knows to be there, everyone shows up, and the show improves every day of every year. Sapient, the technology company I talked about earlier, debriefs at the end of each working day. Debrief while the elements of the mission are *fresh*, and you'll never sacrifice a lesson learned to the vagaries of memory.

5. *Vary the Lead*

Just as we change our flight leads from time to time, you should also change the leadership of your group regularly. Nothing works against "nameless-rankless" faster than an inflexible briefing room hierarchy. Find a method that allows for all the qualified leaders to take turns. Every company should be concerned about nurturing its next generation of leaders, and this is an excellent chance for them to hone their skills.

Don't allow rank to become the sole determinant of who briefs and debriefs your missions. The best executors make the best flight leads, regardless of rank. Vary the lead among your crew members. Allow them to test their ideas. Don't risk the mission, but be just as careful not to create a rank-structured environment *because* of the briefing system.

6. *Go into Detail*

Earlier, we ran quickly through the outlines of typical Air Force briefing and debriefing sessions—but, in truth, what you read on the page was only a quick representation of the level of detail involved in a real briefing. Our briefs are incredibly detailed and absolutely down-to-the-second—and yours should be, too. There are so many ways a flight can go wrong that we turn every mission upside down and shake it hard until we're certain we've left no mistakes in the system. When you analyze the sequence of your mission, you should see as much detail as we do. No, I can't tell you how deep into the details you should go; every situation is different, of course. I can only suggest that it's better to err on the side of too much. Time will tell; if you're spending too much time on unimportant trivia, it'll become obvious pretty quickly. Just remember—the debrief shouldn't be over until you're certain you've nailed the mistakes of one mission and are ready for the next.

MISSION CYCLES

The brief-execute-debrief sequence centers on a definable mission—an event, a task, a process, a sales meeting. You say you don't have definable missions like we do in the sky? Of course you do, but they're not always so obvious—which is why I'll end this section with a few words on defining your mission cycles.

A mission cycle is the period from the start of a mission to its natural ending—in our case, from the brief through the debrief. We've used examples of *events* as missions in this book—major sales presentations, account meetings, brand reviews, annual meetings, shareholder meetings—but every business has definable mission cycles, above and beyond these once-a-month or once-a-year "events." Sometimes it just takes an outsider's perspective to help point them out.

Daily or Weekly Cycles

The first step in defining the mission cycle is to find a pattern of business that you want to isolate as a mission. Certainly it's a matter of choice, but any valid such choice will have some underlying logic to it. Because hotels and inns usually serve traffic on a weekly basis, it might make most sense for them to brief and debrief on a weekly mission cycle. On the other hand, weekends are terribly important in the restaurant business. A brief on Friday morning with a debrief on Sunday night would both prepare the teams for the heavy weekend traffic and include a planned debrief while the team is fresh and the mistakes are vivid.

Other businesses might be better off choosing task-oriented mission cycles. A work contract broken down into daily or weekly milestones can give a complex, long-term process definable, briefable cycles. The new business pitch, for example, can be an excellent, self-contained mission cycle. So, too, are major sales presentations that happen on a frequent, recurring basis, for instance to national account buyers of mass retailers and large chains.

Special Debriefings

In addition to the mission cycles that are defined by the everyday operation of your business, there can and will be special missions requiring their own briefings and debriefings. Consider seasonal changeovers. Almost every class of retailer has seasonal inventory change-outs. Home Depot, for example, has to reset its stores for fall home improvements, just as Neiman-Marcus has to mark down the summer wear and switch over to the fall lines. Home Depot knows that in the fall people want linseed oil–based paints and deck stain, and that the sale and rental of pressure washers will skyrocket as people start washing their decks and restaining them before winter. So Home Depot needs to bring in all its employees and give them a briefing on how to get the store ready to prepare to go into the fall season.

Not Every Mission Can or Should Be Debriefed

This may seem like heresy after all that's come before, but you can't—and shouldn't—debrief everything. In some circumstances, the briefing-debriefing process should be infrequent at most. New salespeople, for example, have so much to learn. They're extremely busy, traveling constantly while learning on the job. A company such as Pfizer sets specific sales call goals for its people each day.

TDI does the same. If each new sales rep briefed and debriefed before and after every call, he'd have no time for selling.

Clearly the most obvious cycle—the sales call itself—is an inappropriate mission cycle for the brief-debrief process. One solution might be to select one day of sales calls per week, define that day as the mission cycle, and put that day through the rigorous process of planning and analysis. If you do this, require your people to brief with you as if they were in the office with you. On the other hand, if your beat is retail rather than wholesale selling, you might find it makes more sense to choose a mission cycle a little more arbitrarily. Home Depot has opted to hold weekly briefings and debriefings. Its basic "squadron" is a store manager and five assistant managers, each of whom represents one of the divisions of the store—lawn and garden, paint, lumber, and so on. Each of the assistant managers has one or two department heads who report to him, and every week they all assemble for briefings and debriefings—in what has proven to be an effective division of the work year and the workforce.

When I was the director of sales and training for Conco, on the other hand, I held monthly sales meetings; that was my mission cycle. My squadron was a regional sales force—usually no more than fifteen people. I briefed very specific mission objectives for every month: Maybe one month we would concentrate on our latex flat paints, to help move out some overstock, and we'd plan a big promotion in our stores; I'd brief the mission, follow the execution, then debrief the results with lessons learned, just as I did for a fighter hop.

Brief-Debrief-Brief

By now you may have hit upon an obvious question—can you combine the briefing with the debriefing? After all, I've given you two examples of weekly mission cycles—a hotel chain and a home-products consumer wholesaler. Would it make sense for companies with such quick cycles to address both briefing and debriefing into one meeting? Absolutely. Following last week's debrief with this week's plan not only saves time—it can help crew members relate lessons learned last week to the assignments of the mission to come.

SUMMARY

The debrief is the mandatory meeting that is held upon completion of a mission, during which the mission participants deconstruct and analyze in detail the mission that just transpired. The objective of the debrief is to pinpoint mistakes made during the mission, identify who made them, and figure out why. Its purpose is not to blame individuals but to improve each member's performance, and the performance of the team.

There are ground rules:

1. The debriefing participants do not pull rank.
2. The debriefing participants are not singled out by name.
3. There is no fear of reprimand in the room.
4. The debrief is led by the pilot who conducted the premission briefing. It has a structure and a sequence:

   a. Briefer restates the mission objective. Were we all clear on this?
   b. Briefer starts to open up lines of communication by first pointing out his own mistakes, then asking participants to critique the motherhood aspects of the mission.
   c. Briefer recaps the entire premission brief. Were we clear on all aspects of it?
   d. Briefer analyzes the mission itself, from beginning to end, and everyone's role in it. Discussion centers first on the mistakes themselves, then on who made them, then on why they were made. The idea here is to learn and improve, not to look for scapegoats.
   e. Briefer recaps the mission outcome. Did we accomplish our main objective? Did we accomplish our secondary objectives?

f. Briefer states the lessons learned, and shares them with other members of the crew.

g. Briefer ends the debrief by emphasizing the positive aspects of the mission.

Follow a similar plan in your business, and you'll find yourself with a team far better equipped to maximize its strengths and improve its weaknesses—an organization bent on success, not just putting in the hours.

12

TOMORROW IS TODAY

Have you ever heard of the Cobra maneuver? I'd be surprised if you had. The Cobra is a radical flight maneuver developed by the Russians. I originally saw it performed a few years ago at an air show by a MiG–29 pilot, but I suspect all the Russian fighter jocks have been trained in it by now. It begins while the MiG is in straight-and-level flight, at a relatively slow speed—say, 250 miles per hour. Without warning, the MiG pilot abruptly pulls back on the stick and the jet snaps straight up in the air, passing through the vertical until the nose is actually leaning backward. As you can imagine, the forward airspeed blends down to almost nothing as the angle of attack increases, and the G forces create drag. However, just before the airspeed is gone, the pilot pushes the nose back down, puts in full afterburner, and reestablishes straight-and-level flight. If you looked at the maneuver from the side and traced it on a piece of paper, you would have drawn a cobra, hood flared and tongue darting in and out of its mouth, ready to bite you in the leg. Which is exactly the purpose of the maneuver. If we'd been engaged in air-to-air combat in a tail chase, I would have flown right past him. One minute he would have been in my gun sights; the next I'd be in *his*.

Boom, I'm dead.

When I saw the Cobra maneuver, I knew a lot of American dog-fighting tactics had just become obsolete. I also knew that some Air Force fighter weapons tactician somewhere was already hard at work analyzing the tapes and trying to figure out a way for our guys to counter the maneuver. In time the results would filter out to the fighter bases, and all the fighter pilots would train in the new countertactics.

The point is, *Tomorrow is today*. Just when you think you're the hottest fighter pilot in the air, along comes a Russian pilot with a maneuver that'll blow you out of the sky.

It's the same in business. Just when you think you've got the perfect customer service people and the best merchandise to offer, along comes a company with better training or a new idea or a better product mix. Your sales start to dip, you start missing quotas, and your management is confused.

How do you avoid the trap? The answer is simple: *Never rest*. Not on your great product. Not on the laurels bestowed on you by your customers. Not on the great training that has turned your sales force into absolute winners. Not on the best debriefs in the business. You have to figure out the chinks in your own armor before others find them for you. And if that means innovating to the point that you render your current product or service obsolete—all the better, for you'll have improved yourself *and* your chances.

Remember again the Persian Gulf War. Even as our F–15s were *dominating* the skies over Iraq, the Air Force was in the process of moving past it, working on the *next* F–15, a jet called the F–22 Raptor. To the forward-thinking planners within the Air Force, despite the incredible success of our pilots, the F–15 was obsolete. It had to go. They had dozens of new fighter jet designs and dozens of new fighter pilot tactics developed; if we didn't get these new ideas into production, the enemy would, and victories like Desert Storm would be a thing of the past.

Case in point: a technology called *vectored thrust*. By attaching powerful vanes to the exhaust of our engines, we can actually vector a jet's thrust—that is, harness, shape, and control it so completely that pilots will be able to fly in a reduced turning radius, add a sideways motion, or even climb *while the jet remains near horizontal to the ground*. Do we have a jet with vectored thrust? Not in production. Can we build one? Yes, we have the technology. Do the Russians have vectored thrust? They didn't during the Gulf War, but they do now. And it's in the air.

Little wonder, then, that while we were winning in the Gulf, chalking up a 100 percent successful engagement record against the most advanced MiGs in the sky, the Air Force was funding the replacement for the F–15s. When the F–22 comes online it will be faster, stealthier, more maneuverable, and filled with more technology than anything I've ever flown. It will be designed to handle new fighter tactics like the Cobra, which will have been flown in experimental aircraft at the Flight Test Center at Edwards AFB. It will make the things I did in the F–15 look like the Wright brothers' first hop.

The point is, even in the midst of the most lopsided air war victory in military history, even in the face of the collapse of the Russian economy, the Air Force wasn't resting on its laurels for even a moment.

Remember, technology changes, and change is constant. If you don't invent it, someone else will. How about your company—are you replacing your product lines with a new and better generation of products and services, or is the competition doing it for you? It's a crucial question, and it goes beyond "new," "improved," and other banalities that lull you into complacency. It involves brutally, unforgivingly, incessantly attacking your own products and services until you find their weaknesses—or, through the process, until you discover untapped market demands. It doesn't mean merely adding line extensions, which may be fine in the short term but ultimately does nothing more than protect the turf you already have (and already may be losing). It means dropping your biases and evaluating your goods and services just as coldly as the consumer does. It means having new product development meetings *without* fixed positions or inflexible points of view already in your mind as you enter the room. Gillette, the world leader in disposable razors, knows this: Despite its huge market share in disposable razors, its razors—and everyone else's—still left a lot to be desired. A lot of product managers might have tried to squeeze another ounce of performance out of the twin-blade concept, but Gillette thought out-of-the-box and came up with a new one—three blades. The introduction of the Mach Three, the product of years of intensive research and testing, has been a smashing success.

The idea of planned obsolescence was perfected in Detroit earlier in this century, and to this day it thrives in the auto industry worldwide. Chrysler is a company peopled with marketing and design geniuses who truly bring an open mind to new-product development; they're excellent at vigorously obsoleting their own product lines. Consider the Dodge Prowler, a car they introduced recently that looks like a cross between a hot-rod Model T and a bumper car from outer space. Is there any other car in dealerships today that looks anything at all like the Prowler? The Dodge boys were thinking ahead—and not surprisingly, the Prowler had a waiting list of eager buyers before it even hit the road.

Procter & Gamble is one of the most consumer-driven companies I have ever seen, and when it comes to self-obsolescence, it rides high on my list. Even before I know enough to worry about some new threat to my teeth—tartar, yellowness, staining—it has a version of Crest on the market designed to meet the challenge. Tartar-Control Crest may compete directly with the regular brand, P&G may lose sales of regular Crest as a result, but it knows the money's going into its pockets and not those of a competitor who thought of the new idea first. The lesson? Cannibalize your own products before others do it for you.

THE PROCESS OF INNOVATION—SOME IDEAS

The strategy of self-obsolescence—of having enough of an open mind to attack your own strengths with radical ideas—may sound easy, but it's not. The first challenge is recognizing ideas for what they are—and what they might become. Let me give you an example of how difficult this is: When the first mainframe computer was built, Tom Watson at Univac (later IBM) was asked by the press to estimate how big the market could possibly be for such behemoth machines. You know his famous answer—they might sell *five*!

Of course, that's the kind of story that makes everyone smirk in hindsight—how could he have failed to foresee the coming computer age? But remember, Watson and his people were brilliant engineers and breakthrough computer designers, not marketing and sales people. Computers were originally developed solely to crunch long number chains and handle mathematical calculations at breakneck speeds, and at that time there weren't a lot of companies that had a pressing need for that capability. Watson was simply viewing their invention from within their own little box. What Watson didn't see—what he wasn't equipped to see—were thousands of ponytailed graphic artists using computers for design and typographic work, thousands of entertainment-industry whiz kids wringing astonishing Hollywood special effects out of their systems, millions of kids playing computer games, and equal numbers of adults processing words and surfing the Web on laptop-size units.

It's not always easy to recognize the commercial viability of a novel idea. But an organization's batting average can be improved if its culture is oriented toward *seeing* ideas. The Air Force is good at this. If the conventional wisdom is to design airplanes with rearward-swept wings, the Air Force will build at least one plane with the wings swept *forward*, just to test the theory. To keep from becoming trapped in circular, in-the-box thinking, it funds something called the Skunk Works. The Skunk Works is actually a design and engineering division of Lockheed-Martin, but unlike the rest of the company, it largely does whatever it pleases, with the blessing of its number one customer—the boys in blue. During World War II, in an era of single-tail, single-engine fighters, the founders of the Skunk Works came up with a slit-tail, twin-engined fighter called the P–38. It was a stunning conceptual leap, and gave our pilots an enormous advantage in air combat. During the Cold War, they envisioned an airplane that could fly so high that no enemy fighter or missile could reach it. The U–2 was born, and it changed intelligence gathering from an art to a science, giving us the ability to look directly down at Soviet targets in real time. Next they designed the stunning SR–71, which I've talked about, and then the fighter that redefined the genre, the stealthy F–117 Nighthawk. (Indeed, so open are Skunk Works engineers to *seeing* novel ideas that they actually saw the idea for the faceted shape of the Stealth in an obscure mathematical formula developed by a Russian theorist. The Russians ignored the model; the Skunk Works people built the Stealth. And the Stealth was on the flight line six years before it was needed in combat—how's that for self-obsolescing!)

Some companies are better at seeing new ideas than others. 3M is among the best. Not only does it encourage the entrepreneurial spirit in its employees, and allow for "think time" to help them brainstorm, it takes the necessary risk when it sees the germ of a commercial idea—it puts the product in test markets. Post-It Notes are the quintessential example of this. They came about by accident, a by-product of a search for a different type of adhesive—but 3M recognized their utility, and the rest is history.

TOMORROW'S REVENUES WILL COME FROM PRODUCTS YOU DON'T MAKE TODAY

How important is the concept of "tomorrow is today"? Most companies derive a significant portion of their revenues from products or services that didn't even exist five years ago. Marriott, largely a traditional hotel company, could ill-afford to stand on the sidelines as the growth in all-suites hotels—a new concept—steadily leached market share away from traditional hotels; after examining the competition, it designed its own all-suites line, Residence Inns, and established a thriving subdivision. Intel launches new computer chips on an almost monthly basis. And as soon as the nineteen-inch monitor was *it* in the industry, along came flat-screen monitors to make them look old and clunky. New golf clubs, new tennis racquets, new snow skis, new breakfast cereals, new washing powders, new menu items, new retail chains, faster modems—the entire concept of innovation is essential to tomorrow's revenues.

At its optimal level, this forward-thinking strategy should keep you not one but *two* steps ahead of the competition, leapfrogging ahead of them by developing products one generation forward of *their* response to you. How does this work? The F–117 is a good example. The

F–117 Stealth fighter is designed to be invisible to conventional radar; the Air Force is so certain its technology works that it trains pilots to fly straight and level, right past the paths of guided missiles zooming by their windshields. In any other jet, the pilot would be yanking and banking left and right to shake off his radar lock. Not the F–117 pilot: He flies straight and level because the missiles can't see him—and believe me, that takes incredible nerve!

But here's the thing: The Air Force doesn't allow itself to believe even for a moment that the F–117 will remain radar-invisible forever. In fact, it knows the opposite is true—sooner or later, someone will come up with a way to outwit it. Technology is a competitive game, a volley of shifting advantage; if you're smart you can get ahead, but only for a short time, and then someone else will charge past you. The Air Force knew that the day it used the F–117 publicly, as it did in the Gulf War, would be the beginning of its end. It knew that the Russians and the Chinese—and probably the French and the Germans, too—would leap into high gear to find the weaknesses in its capability.

Did knowing this worry the Air Force? Not at all. Its engineering teams had already been looking for the flaws, developing the fixes, and looking for flaws yet again. By the time Stealth counter-measures are deployed, the Air Force will have moved on to a newer technology.

Are any of your engineers shooting down your products? Well, they should be. Someone, somewhere, is going to come up with a better idea for your flagship products—and he might as well be working for you.

SMOKING HOLES

The alternatives to lagging in marketplace are dire. There are smoking holes out on the corporate landscape today because companies didn't push the envelope fast enough and stay ahead, or at least preserve their advantages—Vuarnet sunglasses, Hayes modems, even the mighty Apple Computers came close.

It's a lesson we in the Air Force live with every day: You can never rest. You can never assume that today's fighter jet will be tomorrow's victor in the sky. The finality of air combat drives the Air Force to innovate, to experiment, to see the potential in oddball ideas, whether they originate on an engineer's drawing table or in an obscure Russian mathematical formula. The business of combat demands no less—you, no less than we, must strive to innovate, to challenge your products, to *see* new ideas—always with a sharp eye on the attitude indicator and a cross-check that helps you recognize the next opportunity.

SUMMARY

The business landscape is dynamic, just like the modern battlefield. Nothing stays the same for long. The only way to compete and execute on the cutting edge is to innovate so thoroughly that even your own products and services will eventually become obsolete. If you don't, some company you've never heard of will reach the market with your product—in an improved version. Or it'll leapfrog your product altogether and offer a product that is a generation ahead. Every company should work as hard as possible to preserve and grow its market share—because if someone else starts eating away at that share, it can be next to impossible to regain it. Here's how to keep it from happening:

1. Improve your product constantly.

2. Look over the horizon and reinvent your product completely if you have to.

3. Think out of the box to create new uses or applications for your products.

4. Remember that tomorrow is today: The products and services that will bankrupt your company are out there on somebody's drawing board—*right now*.

13

PEOPLE

The magic ingredient in any organization is its people. People can be as mercurial, as vibrant and surprising and unpredictable and difficult to manage, as alchemy. We are all prone to streaks of brilliance, and yet easily vulnerable to failings. So much of what we call corporate success rides on the powerful performance of each of us as individuals. The Air Force can teach me to fly and give me exhaustive training, but my performance will still be colored by mysterious elements of timing and circumstance—the X factors, if you will. Will I get brain lock? Will I panic? Will I perform brilliantly? Or will I have a turn of bad luck?

This book began with people and it ends with people, because ultimately they are an organization's greatest asset. It is individuals who innovate, not companies. It is individuals who persist against all odds, not corporate guidelines or a time clock. Individuals overcome odds and turn flat projections into stunning sales victories, not corporate mission statements. Ask economists why a company grew faster than projected or avoided a downturn that seemed inevitable, and they will invariably cite the unpredictable nature of entrepreneurship—of *people*. Fred Smith of FedEx is famous for having defied the onset of a financial crisis by wining a payroll's worth of money at the gambling tables of Las Vegas. Find a management book with a chapter on *that!*

The Air Force focuses its assets like the shaft of a spear behind those who execute the mission—its people. At the pointy end is a fantastic piece of technology, a tremendous amount of training, the efforts of maintainers, weaponeers, controllers, and briefers—and the pilot. Not that any one person can lay claim to a victory. Not that any mission is a solo ride. But, in the end, only one person handles the flight controls, only one person asks for the sale, only one person talks to the customer, only one person has the big idea. One person, one transaction, one customer at a time—that's the underlying force of companies big and small. And when it works, it's because each individual person executes brilliantly.

When a company puts its focus on execution, things begin to *happen*—and the results appear before the naked eye. You see them putting your product on the shelves in the supermarkets, you see customers in your store, you see hotel guests checking in, and you hear your phone ringing with new orders. Execution-oriented companies and execution-oriented people put things in motion, put deals into play—*they get things done*. They're not always right, but they act decisively, and they have feedback loops—such as the mission debrief—to correct the problems when things go wrong.

The creation of an execution-oriented culture is a fundamental key to success—and an essential if you want to attract good people. Employees who learn to execute are often impatient with management that lags behind them: "Give us cell phones so we can reschedule faster," cries one sales force. "I need a scanner and fax/modem," says a route driver delivering potato chips. Fail to meet the demands of an eager workforce, fail to rise to the challenge of eager people who are impatient to execute, and you will find eager workers abandoning you for the company that will. Fail to support the customer service force with exemplary products, top-notch competitive research, and the tools to meet customer demands, and they'll leave you to work for the company that does.

People. *Executors*. These must be your company's number one priority. Not only should they have every support possible—from training and tools, to new products and services to market—but when they do you'll find they will help the company build in ways you never anticipated.

It's no different in the Air Force.

The satisfaction of brilliant execution, of being on a winning team, of having the latest, hottest jet in the sky—these are the things that make fighter pilots proud as they stand beside their jets at air shows. You can tell that these people *want* to be a part of the organization. They wear their uniforms proudly.

Is your company attracting good people? And are you able to keep them? Are they given a sense of mission, and do they feel empowered to hold up their end? Management's job is to make good people feel at home in the company. To make them feel wanted, empowered, and successful. In return, good people will stretch your company's boundaries in all the right directions. They will push everyone to innovate and improve not just the things in their own camp—but to improve the products and services of the entire company. You will feel no small measure of bottom-up pushing for excellence when you have the right people on your team. Embrace them. Respond to them. Rise to them.

People want to be winners, and they have a bottomless ability to make success happen. Ultimately, that is what makes the Air Force's regimen of training and personal development work—people will push themselves beyond the ordinary limits when they believe in what they are doing. The Air Force takes that desire and focuses it, molds it, gives it the tools and the techniques needed to make a winner.

Now you have those tools, too. You've learned the value of camaraderie, teamwork, and common goals. You've acquired an appreciation for personal discipline and attention to detail, a sense of the importance of duty and personal confidence. If you can implement this book's lessons in your company, chances are your people will learn to support its people more effectively as they execute their missions. They'll learn to set mission objectives and integrate their crews into each mission by creating a comprehensive mission plan. They'll learn to bring the details of the mission to everyone through a mission brief, and to empower people through the execution phase by giving them the tools to avoid the dangers of task saturation and improve their performance. Finally, those who execute the mission have learned the value of debriefing as a way to improve day after day after day.

And when all that is done, what you'll have on your hands is a company that's remaking itself every day—relentlessly re-creating its products, refining its services, and improving the performance of its individual members. A company that, in short, is perfectly poised to win each new battle it confronts—to achieve victory in the combat of business.

I know you can do it, because I've done it myself.

INDEX